Transforming the Legacy: People of Spirit in the 21st Century

Volume I: The Legacy and the Challenges

A Symposium held at Wesley Theological Seminary

Washington DC

December 17-19, 2009

E. Maynard Moore, Content Editor

M. George Walters, Technical Editor

www.ResurgencePublishing.com

Dean -
With appreciation
of your leadership
Maynard
Sept. 15, 2010

Transforming the Legacy: People of Spirit in the 21st Century

Published with Permission: The original materials used in this publication are provided by the authors. All editing of those materials is the responsibility of the editors of this publication and in no way is intended to represent the views or opinions of those who contributed originals or copies of the materials.

Info@ResurgencePublishing.com

www.ResurgencePublishing.com

Cover design by Richard G. Walters

Cover graphic from the photography of George Ensinger

ISBN 0-9763892-4-X

Printed in the United States of America

Table of Contents

Table of Contents

Background

Purpose of the Symposium

To commemorate the 2009 opening of the Joseph Wesley Mathews Archives at the Wesley Theological Seminary Library, publicizing the archives availability for graduate student research, and to promote the legacy of Bishop James K. Mathews and Dean Joseph Wesley Mathews as their ministries continue to inspire and guide People of the Spirit in the 21st Century.

The Honorees

Left Joseph Wesley Mathews; Right Eunice & James K. Mathews

Visit the Symposium Website Photo Gallery to see pictures of

Joe and Lyn Mathews over their years together: See

Http://www.ResurgencePublishing.com

Joseph Wesley Mathews

October 8, 1911 – October 16, 1977

Joe was born in Breezewood, Pennsylvania, the fifth child and second son of James Davenport Mathews and Laura Mae Wilson Mathews, a small town in the Tuscarora Mountains where his father was supply pastor of the Methodist Episcopal Church. The family was marked by a strong religious heritage, "shouting Methodists" of Scotch-Irish extraction with roots in England and Wales. Laura Mae's forebears hailed from Ulster, and had migrated to the Ohio Valley. The family prized education, including Bible school every Sunday.

Joe grew up in Ada, Ohio, where the family had settled for a while following father James' itinerant appointments to small churches. After a brief sojourn in Houston, the family moved back to Ohio, this time to Mansfield, where Joe graduated from high school exactly at the onset of the Great Depression. Without money for college, and with little income from short-term jobs, Joe got into theater, and was serious enough about acting that he even, for a time, went to Hollywood. But the Christian message was too strong to resist, and by 1932 Joe found himself at Lincoln Memorial University in Tennessee, where brother Jim had already enrolled. There the two brothers excelled, and spent the summers intensively involved in evangelism, preaching throughout the small towns in the Cumberland Mountains. They each matriculated in turn to New York Theological Seminary, but Joe transferred after two years to Drew University, where he received his Divinity degree *cum laude* in 1939. While studying part-time at Union Theological Seminary under Paul Tillich, and serving a small church in Sharon, Connecticut, Joe met Evelyn Johnston, and they were married January 3, 1942, in Wilmington, Delaware, Lyn's hometown.

WW II and Pearl Harbor affected Joe deeply, and in spring 1942, Joe volunteered for service in the U.S. Army, and on May 5, was commissioned as a Chaplain. He served with distinction for almost four years in the Pacific Theatre, being awarded the Bronze Star for his work under heavy enemy fire as his unit stormed the islands of the South Pacific. In one day he pronounced benedictions over 4,000 being buried in mass graves. These years marked Joe for the rest of his life; he was deactivated December 31, 1945.

Joe resumed his studies at Yale Divinity School, under the tutelage of H. Richard Niebuhr, who became the most potent influence in his theological awakening. By 1947 he was accepted as a Ph.D. candidate, and though he completed a 400-page dissertation, by now he was headed in a different direction. With additions to the family, Joe and Lyn moved first to Colgate, where he taught for three years, and by 1952, he accepted an appointment to teach at Perkins School of Theology in Dallas. This chapter ended in 1956 when Joe went to Austin to join Jack Lewis at the new Christian Faith and Life Community, a laboratory of serious Christian living and education for lay leaders, intent on the renewal of the Church in America. By 1959, they had developed the "daily office," which remained central to the enterprise for decades.

In 1962, a number of the families joined Joe and Lyn with their family – Joe Jr., James and John -- as he accepted the call to provide leadership as

Dean of the Ecumenical Institute in Evanston, Illinois, which had been transferred from the World Council of Churches to the auspices of the Greater Chicago Church Federation. First from the one-house Evanston campus, and then the Bethany campus on Chicago's West Side where Fifth City was born, and then from the Kemper campus on North Sheridan Road, Joe and his colleagues, peaking at nearly 2000 strong, set about changing the world. The end for Joe came in the fall of 1977. His legacy is now in our hands.

James Kenneth Mathews

Bishop Earl G. Hunt, Jr. once wrote of his colleague: "Jim Mathews tells about the yesterdays but still lives deliberately in the tomorrows. He is, indeed, 'a pilgrim of the future,' to borrow Pierre Teilhard de Chardin's fascinating self-description." Few of us would disagree with that apt summation. Jim entered the world on February 10, 1913, in Breezewood, Pennsylvania, making him some 15 months the junior to his brother Joe, and, as he reminds us, just about three weeks prior to Woodrow Wilson's first inauguration. Joe and Ken (as he was called in those days) came of age in Ada, Ohio, where the family had relocated, but each of the brothers graduated high school in Mansfield, in June 1930. Both had to work for a year before entering college, and while Joe went for a time to Hollywood, Jim enrolled at Lincoln Memorial University where one could work to cover all expenses, and in 33 months, had earned a baccalaureate degree.

By then Joe had rejoined his brother, and they secured a license to preach, issued in the Holston Conference, and Jim enrolled in Biblical Theological Seminary in New York, where Joe joined him two years later. There they were taught a rigorous inductive method of Bible study that required an extensive method of charting, typically from left to right, and though Jim utilized this method of study the rest of his life, Joe developed the method to a fine art. In May 1937, Jim was received as a trial member of the New York Conference; Bishop Francis McConnell ordained him a deacon. Jim enrolled in a program of graduate study at Boston University School of Theology, but when he heard a presentation by Bishop Azariah, the first Indian to be elected bishop in the Anglican communion, he changed his course and within three months found himself, ill-prepared as he felt, on his way to India as a missionary, ending up as a pastor in Bombay.

It was in nearby Poona, almost a year later, that Jim met the great missionary evangelist E. Stanley Jones, and friends schemed to introduce him to Dr. Jones' daughter Eunice, who was traveling with him as his secretary. In Jim's words, immediately he was "smitten when Eunice walked into the room," and they managed to meet "again, and again, and again." On June 1, 1940, they were married in the chapel of the Wellesley School in Naini Tal. By 1942, the world was at war, and Jim volunteered, finding himself soon appointed First Lieutenant in the Army's Quartermaster Corps, and assigned to Karachi. He was to serve four years in the China-Burma-India Theater, but never witnessed the wrenching scenes of combat and death in the Western Pacific as did brother Joe.

At war's end, Jim and Eunice returned to the States, where he was to serve the next 14 years as associate general secretary of the Division of World Mission of the Board of Missions of the Methodist Church (today's General Board of Global Ministries). Jim completed his Ph.D. work at Columbia University in the field of History of Religion. He began to write, and traveled extensively to Methodist outposts around the world. In 1956, he was elected a bishop by the conference in Lucknow, but declined the position, insisting that they select a native-born leader for that responsibility. Four years later, he again was elected Bishop, this time in the Northeastern Jurisdiction, and was consecrated to the post in the National Church of United Methodism in Washington DC, Metropolitan Memorial.

Newly-minted bishop Jim and Eunice were assigned to the Boston area, where they provided leadership for the next 12 years. Another eight years brought him back to the national capital area. Retirement was mandatory in 1980, but with experience too valuable to ignore, he subsequently served "interim" appointments as the presiding Episcopal leader in Zimbabwe (where he set the stage for the founding of Africa University), the Albany Area in New York, and finally in New York City. As a result, Bishop James K. Mathews holds the distinction of having served as the Episcopal leader of ten Annual Conferences, more than any person in the history of United Methodism. Today he holds the honorary position of "Bishop-in-Residence" at Metropolitan Memorial in Washington, DC, and resides with Eunice in Bethesda, Maryland.

Introduction

E. Maynard Moore, Ph.D. on behalf of the Organizing Committee

This book was conceived as part of the original plan of the organizing committee that put together the components of the Symposium in December 2009 in Washington DC. The event was hosted by Wesley Theological Seminary as the natural venue for lifting up the heritage of two brothers in the faith: Joseph Wesley Mathews and James K. Mathews.

In the previous year, the Seminary had responded to an initial inquiry on the part of the two sons of Joseph Mathews, as these brothers sought a permanent place for their father Joe's private papers. The academic dean of the Seminary at that time, Dr. Bruce C. Birch, and the Seminary President David McAllister-Wilson, actively facilitated the transfer of the papers from Chicago, and the Director of the Library at Wesley Seminary, Dr. William Faupel, personally drove a rented truck with two student interns to transport the file boxes back to Washington.

The goal of the Symposium was two-fold: to lift up the heritage of the two Mathews brothers for the new generation of scholars and students, and secondly, to generate enough financial support to initiate the cataloguing of the papers into an archive for research in urban ministry. The two goals dovetail nicely with a current high priority of Wesley Theological Seminary, which has initiated a far-sighted academic program in urban ministry that promises to break new ground in modeling ministry in the 21st century.

Motivating the organizing committee to hurry rather than tarry, Bishop James K. Mathews and his wife Eunice gave us moral and financial support from the beginning.

Though recovering from a stroke suffered three years previously, Bishop Mathews gained enough strength by December 2009 to grace the gathered participants with his presence at the Symposium, and at one point riveted the attention of all 150 persons when he rose to his feet and commended their commitments to ministry in all corners of the globe.

We were enormously gratified by the fact that eight of the ten Annual Conferences in the Northeastern Jurisdiction of the United Methodist Church provided generous financial support for the Symposium as well. This permitted us to keep the registration fee unusually low, but that was a necessity since the people who carry on the heritage of the Mathews brothers are spread around the world carrying out ministry by the bootstraps in distressed urban centers and remote rural villages. It also allowed us to register a small number of current seminary students for a token fee.

Early in 2009, the organizing committee made a list of potential speakers for the Symposium, and again we were gratified that every one of those we invited to participate did so, contributing their speeches to the participants represented in the manuscripts that now comprise this book. December weather delayed planes and the heaviest snow in the history of the nation's capital delayed half of the participants in their planned departures. Bishop Schol arrived from the airport just minutes before his opening address. Bishop Weaver had to turn around on his trek south and return to New England when the weather became too hazardous for travel. Bishop May and his wife changed their plans so that he could accommodate our request that he speak at the opening session, and managed to get home ahead of the storm. Bishop Susan Morrison was not so lucky and shared the fate of those stranded at the hotel on the last day. To all of these persons, and to the others who provided leadership, the committee is extremely grateful.

The heart of the Symposium could be found in the dialogue groups that were organized along six specific topical tracks. The deans of each of the six tracks did a masterful job of coordinating the presentations, and facilitating the discussions. This was no small feat, because at one point on the second day, as the storm gathered strength outside, the power went off in the northwest DC neighborhood where the Seminary is located. This became just a minor barrier to be overcome, and perhaps because there were no power point presentations to be generated, some of the best discussions transpired that morning.

Not all of the speakers produced manuscripts for inclusion in this volume, but those who did so are well represented here. We have included a couple of additional pieces that did not find an opening for presentation in the gerrymandered schedule, and several others have been expanded and reformatted for reading rather than hearing. In addition, Part One of this volume contains two pieces by the two Mathews brothers that have not been previously published.

The first is a paper out of the Joe Mathews archives at Wesley Seminary. It is an address called "Resurgement and the Religious," and was given at the closing plenary session of the Guardians' Meeting in Chicago on April 13-15, 1973. It is a call for what Dean Joe called "awakenment," which in his mind functioned as the state of justification – the full sense of humanness that should characterize our intentional mission. "Resurgement" was the word he used for sanctification, which for him meant living in a dynamical state of happening – otherwise known as resurrection. It is my feeling that this paper needs to be "re-discovered" for those who make claims to be part of the ongoing People of Spirit in the 21st century, which is what the Symposium was all about.

The second paper is actually the last sermon that Bishop James K. Mathews preached prior to his stroke on 2005, preached in my hearing at Metropolitan Memorial United Methodist Church in Washington DC, where Bishop Mathews and his wife Eunice continue their long-standing affiliation. I express my thanks to his daughter, Anne Mathews-Younes, who helped recover this text from the few remaining files in her parents' home. It is significant that this sermon, preached on September 25, 2005, came just after the disaster of Hurricane Katrina, and just as the surge of troops were being deployed to Iraq. One could easily discern the emotion that Bishop Mathews was exhibiting that day, and his call was compelling for us all to be sensitive to the subtleties of the conditions in which the poor and marginalized find themselves trapped.

None of us knew at the time, of course, that it would be the last time he would stand in the pulpit, but it now is a fitting expression of the caring commitment he demonstrated throughout his long ministry for the "left-outs" of the world.

The papers in Part Two are compelling in their own way. There is recognition of the heritage of the two Mathews brothers, of course – that was the context in which everyone spoke. But most of the content of these papers is forward-looking: challenging us to build on that heritage, and to recover the sense of urgency that the two Mathews brothers demonstrated in caring for those they served. We have a lot to learn from what they bequeath to us. Each of the speakers and the workshop leaders, even when one might not have known either brother personally (though most did), forcefully picks up on one or another thread of the Symposium theme, and spoke from the gut, as it were.

Bishop John Schol, dashing in from the airport to the opening session, welcomed everyone to Washington DC. Serving as he does as the presiding Bishop of the Baltimore-Washington Annual Conference of the United Methodist Church, he brings his own long experience in urban ministry to the podium. In the context of the specific ministries of the two Mathews brothers, he laid out how the priorities of the Baltimore-Washington Conference, where Bishop Mathews served for the last eight years before his retirement in 1980, are expressions of that vision which we all here inherit. He laid before us a powerful foundation on which all of the other speakers could build.

Bishop Felton Edwin May, who retired from the active episcopacy in 2004 after serving twenty years on three separate assignments, picked up immediately on the Symposium theme. Bishop May continues in a very active leadership role as the Executive Director of the Multi-Ethnic Center for Urban Ministry in the Northeastern Jurisdiction of the United Methodist Church, which means he is immersed in ministry issues in most of the major cities in the eastern corridor of the United States. He spoke in a compelling manner as to how both Joe Mathews and Jim Mathews shaped his own life and ministry.

The keynote address came from the Rev. Dr. William A. Holmes, who served for twenty-four years as senior minister at Metropolitan Memorial Church in Washington DC, the National Church of United Methodism. Holmes intrigued everyone with an account of his first day in seminary in the 1950s as he sat in Joe Mathews' class for first year students at Perkins. He spent the next 20 years as a minister in Texas, and was one of the master teachers for the Christian Faith and Life Institute in Austin. Later, of course, it was Bishop Jim Mathews who called Holmes to the pastorate in the nation's capital. He continues to teach lay study courses even today in congregations, with people who do not recognize that they are getting RS-1. He presented a strong challenge to those gathered at the Symposium.

Rabbi Fred Scherlinder Dobb made the kick-off presentation in the Environmental/Ecology track, and had all who participated enthralled with the idea of "sacred space." The presentation influenced every aspect of the subsequent discussion the rest of the weekend. The same could be said of some of the other workshop presentations, and several of those are presented in the chapters that follow. Dr. Fred Smith and Dr. Sam Marullo, who lead the intensive course of study in Urban Ministry at Wesley Theological Seminary, provided the framework for all of the discussions in that track. When reading those and the several additional papers, one can easily see how the workshop participants were enriched with new ideas and challenged to develop strategies for action.

Bishop James K. Mathews was one of three faith leaders who, in 1978, began to discuss the need for an interfaith association in the nation's capital. He and colleagues Cardinal William Baum and Episcopal Bishop John T. Walker issued appropriate invitations, and by year's end, they were joined by prominent Jewish and Islamic leaders to sign a cooperative agreement that formed the InterFaith Conference of Metropolitan Washington. Not only is the IFC the oldest and one of the largest such organizations in the country, it now numbers eleven faith groups in collaborative projects to promote dialogue, interfaith understanding, social justice and religious freedom. Bishop Mathews, who is now the sole survivor among the original signatories, has been honored by IFC and other groups for his pioneering work in this field. Clark Lobenstine, IFC Executive Director for over 30 years, in his paper presented here, tells this compelling story.

The paper authored by Dr. E. Maynard Moore was not presented at the Symposium, but was written with that possibility in mind had there been a last-minute cancellation with a slot to fill. The paper picks up on the important study of theological education supervised and coordinated by Dr. H. Richard Niebuhr, who was the primary mentor for Joe Mathews and his dissertation advisor at Yale Divinity School. Seminary education has changed in the decades since the Niebuhr commission made its recommendations, but the question remains: have the connections between seminary and congregation changed, and if so, in what ways? Dr. Moore raises implicit questions from Niebuhr's themes for a doctrine of the church, and suggests some ways that we can apply these insights if we are to be People of Spirit in the 21st century, as our theme implies.

Bishop Susan M. Morrison, whose ministry was shaped by Bishop Mathews' Episcopal leadership, expanded on her short introduction to the book Eternal Values in a World of Change. Bishop Mathews wrote this book for the Women's Division of Christian Service of the Board of Missions of the former Methodist Church in 1959. Long out of print, Resurgence Publishing has issued a 2nd edition in 2009, with an addendum of Bishop Mathews "valedictory" address to the Northeastern Jurisdiction upon his retirement in 1980. Bishop Morrison outlined its major points and showed how she learned how to study theology as a pastor under Bishop Mathews using charting methodologies that are familiar to us all.

The final chapter in this volume is the presentation by Dr. Bruce C. Birch, the Dean Emeritus at Wesley Theological Seminary, and was intended as the closing address at the Symposium until the record snowfall required schedule adjustments. It remains a fitting close to this volume, as Dr. Birch rehearses the impact that both Joe Mathews and Jim Mathews had on his career, the former through E.I. colleagues in Iowa in the 1960s and the latter as Bishop in the national capital area. Through his long tenure as Dean at Wesley, Dr. Birch observed practices and principles in seminary education throughout the country, and has had a strong, influential role in shaping Wesley as a global seminary for the 21st century. This paper goes a long way toward giving us direction in the decade ahead.

It is our hope that this volume will do more than recapitulate what transpired at the Symposium in December 2009. From the beginning we intended to present this volume as a means to impel those in attendance to move forward on some of the strategies discussed, and to provide momentum for the movement "in formation" called the "Springboard" network. Those in that network have a common heritage that traces back to Joseph W. Mathews and James K. Mathews, but it is much more than that. Others must be brought into the movement, for the principles we have learned are alive and quite relevant for the needs of the world to which the church is called to minister.

In fact, it is more often than not that those who are "out in the world" are most readily recognized as "People of Spirit" in our time. There are some of those in our midst. The question is (for those of us in the church) – what do we have to bring to the table? Are we yet alive?

Acknowledgments of Support

The organizers of the Symposium wish to express our deep appreciation to all who attended the sessions in December and who contributed their insights and gifts to make it a success. All who participated recognized the high level of enthusiasm and spirit that was exhibited in all of the discussions. Especially we want to thank the President of Wesley Theological Seminary, all of the staff that was involved, and in particular the coordination on-site provided by the Director of the Library, Dr. D. William Faupel, in whose care the Joseph Wesley Archives now reside. Within the next 18 to 24 months the archival center should be in place and the papers will be open to researchers and scholars.

In addition, we are deeply grateful for the Bishops of the Northeastern Jurisdiction of the United Methodist Church who, individually and in the face of serious budget challenges, somehow found enough funds from their stretched budgets to make end-of-year gifts that allowed us to move forward with our plans. Similarly, the leadership of several congregations responded generously to our requests, and we extend to them our sincere thanks. May we all move forward now – not just to extend the heritage but to expand the ministry and vision of the Mathews brothers to the generations to come.

Finally, we are deeply indebted to Jim and Betty Ann Angel, experienced publishers, now retired, members of Metropolitan Memorial United Methodist Church, who read the entire manuscript and provided detailed editorial changes and suggestions in order to get spoken presentations into formats suitable for the printed page. We extend our appreciation to them far beyond this simple word of thanks.

The Organizing Committee

Susan F. Craver
D. William Faupel, Ph.D.
Jack C. Gilles
E. Maynard Moore, Ph.D.
M. George Walters, M. Div.

Acknowledgment and Appreciation

We are deeply grateful for the support that has been provided by agencies of the United Methodist Church, by individuals who support this vision, and by several other institutions who join us as partners.

- **Metropolitan Memorial Cooperative Parish, Washington DC**
  - Metropolitan Memorial United Methodist Church
  - St. Luke's United Methodist Church
  - Wesley United Methodist Church
- **Annual Conferences in the Northeastern Jurisdiction**
  - Central Pennsylvania Annual Conference
  - Eastern Pennsylvania Annual Conference
  - Greater New Jersey Annual Conference
  - New England Annual Conference

  - New York Annual Conference
  - New York West Episcopal Area
  - Western Pennsylvania Annual Conference
  - West Virginia Annual Conference
- **Foundry United Methodist Church, Washington DC**
- **Wesley Theological Seminary, Washington DC**

The following individuals and friends:

- Marilyn and Joe Crocker
- Jack and Judy Gilles
- Lela Jahn
- Dr. & Mrs. William A. Holmes
- Charles A. Lingo, Jr.
- Bishop & Mrs. James K. Mathews
- Mr. & Mrs. William C. Parker, Jr.
- Bill Parker
- James Wiegel

Prelude

David McAllister-Wilson, President, Wesley Theological Seminary

"The world will little note, nor long remember what we say here." That sentiment from Lincoln's Gettysburg Address captures the nagging fear of every academic symposium, every speech and sermon, and, indeed, of every archivist. There is a theory of history that there are only impersonal tides in the affairs of men and women; that forces of geography and climate, economy and genes and chance determine the course of events. If so, we as individuals are but flotsam and jetsam riding the troughs and waves. Then, there is what used to be called the "Great Man" theory of history, which says that certain individual people can make waves and that committed and concerted action matters.

Joe Mathews made waves. It was a remarkable testimony to the force of this man's life and work that over 30 years after his death 150 people came to Washington from all over the world and stayed for dialogue, despite a major snow storm. They came not just to honor the memory or engage in nostalgia. As the name of the symposium indicates, they wanted to see the legacy of Joe Mathews and the Ecumenical Institute transformed in order to be a blessing to the 21th century.

I am grateful to the organizers of the symposium, especially to Dr. Maynard Moore whose efforts made this possible, and to the speakers who challenged us at every turn. But most especially, I'm grateful to those who attended. They "stormed" the seminary with their determined spirit and helped us dedicate the establishment of the Joseph W. Mathews Archive at Wesley Theological Seminary.

Prelude

The papers, speeches and documents associated with Joe Mathews' life work are boxed as a unit, the whole being assigned to the care of Dr. D. William Faupel, Director of the Libraries and Archives at the Seminary. I believe a seminary library is the best location for this resource and I pledge that we will be good stewards. I think a seminary is founded on a "great person" theory of history. I refer not only to the life and work of the "one who became flesh and dwelt among us," but also to the history of the Body of Christ. By the urging of the Holy Spirit, individual men and women answering a call to ministry have salted history with the message of the Gospel and worked for the Kingdom of God to come on earth. Any seminary ought to be feeding a steady stream of these change agents into the world.

Wesley Theological Seminary is distinctively suited for this mission. We were brought to Washington in 1958 by a Methodist Bishop who was determined that there be a Methodist seminary in Washington. Bishop G. Bromley Oxnam began his ministry in the early days of the 20th century. Just like Joe Mathews would do a generation later in Chicago, Oxnam pioneered a new kind of urban ministry in Los Angeles. That experiment became the Church of All Nations and was replicated in other cities nationwide. Oxnam then became involved in global issues with relief efforts during and after both World Wars. He was elected Bishop and ultimately appointed to the Washington Area. He moved Wesley to our present campus so that we might be engaged in the city and become a truly global seminary. Because of one man's vision and initiative, all of these things have become true for Wesley and we grew from being a small seminary in Maryland to being one of the largest and most diverse seminaries in the world. Bromley Oxnam's ashes are buried in the chapel on campus named for him, and Joe Mathews' archive will rest literally next to Oxnam's papers in the library.

The timing is providential. This archive of the record of a Chicago community organizer was established in the inaugural year of another Chicago community organizer: President Barack Obama. And, this is the year when we have established a major new presence in downtown Washington. Wesley at Mt. Vernon Square is a partnership between the seminary, a historically black United Methodist Church, and the former flagship of the southern Methodist church. It will serve as the headquarters for a major expansion of our programs in urban ministry and public theology. And, in this facility, we have established an intentional living community of students. In many ways, what we are setting out to accomplish is the next iteration of the vision of Joe Mathews.

It is no small coincidence that Washington and Wesley are "home" to Joe's brother, Bishop James K. Mathews. Jim Mathews also served as Bishop of the Washington Area and worked to make sure Wesley stayed true to the vision of our placement in Washington. Later, as Bishop-in-Residence and a member of our faculty, he did much to nurture this institution. In the Mathews brothers, we see lived examples of the soul of Methodism: the twining of personal and social holiness. Incised on the cornerstone of the library is the Charles Wesley line that describes their commitment to both the life of the mind and the way of the heart: "Unite the pair so long disjoined, knowledge and vital piety."

Inside this library, then, are not just papers of antiquarian interest for the caretakers of antique churches. Instead, we intend it to be an active resource for seminary students, scholars, and lay people who will study the life and work of Joe Mathews not just to know who he was, but to ask: "how did he do it?" We gratefully receive this potent collection as a blessing to this seminary community in the prayer that it will help us be a blessing to the world through the church.

Remarks by Joseph A. Slicker

From his current home in Dallas, Texas

The Washington Symposium is a wonderful plan and happening. It will be a great celebration of Joe Mathews' works inaugurating his Archives for posterity, without which there would have been no Order as we know it. Also it will be a great celebration of the work of all of us that have continued the journey. Honor each one and every happening that has taken place in our individual and collective lives. Celebrate the sacredness of who you/we are. Take it into your heart with joy and gratitude as you feel full of celebration.

Now as you turn to some planning, drop all the past and turn to what, if I remember correctly, Martin Luther King called, ***'The Fierceness of the Now'***. It's the only habitat of the Spirit -- Life itself. There is nowhere else to go or live. It is the empty space of the no-longer and the not-yet. That must be our only home and our base of operations. The Now feeds the not-yet, as it carries out the inner dialogue with the next creative moment.

Now we begin to understand that the external world for us is only going to change as we change our inner world. We are here to finally clean-up our lives, our separation from ourselves, others, and the All -- sometimes, bit by bit. Perhaps, for the first time, we live in a time that it is possible to see our living relationship and obligation to love nature and the Cosmos as a whole.

As you look to the clash of values and the utter ambiguity of every situation, we can never claim or justify that we are uninvolved or not responsible. The starving, the dispossessed, the injured, the wronged, and the brain-washing of...all of us... by the material myth of the so-called

'American Dream' or 'La Dolce Vita' or striving for our own benefit at the expense of others. The fact that we can be aware of all this is, perhaps, our first step into living today in the not-yet of the Now of the radical revolution today.

The gift to every human is the Being-Becoming pair of opposites. These opposites are eternally attached – they are inseparable. Recall that the Being side is the formless and can only be approached through stillness, emptiness or nothingness, sheer blank empty space. The Becoming side is form, the external, the everyday life. The form is fed by the formless at every moment, every Now. It is the gift of Eternal Life, of being Alive, of Being filled with the Spirit. And still we forsake our calling to be who we are, our sacredness. The Now, the not-yet, is the entrance that explodes this moment. Thus, to get to, or change what appears as the external, we have to go through the Now, our Being side.

Close your eyes and look inward. Watch what is going on...not what you may think is going on. Let go of your thinking and feeling as best you can. Let your body relax. Be still outwardly and inwardly. Watch what is going on. Use Contemplative Prayer or Meditation to observe what is taking place in your inner space. Just stay with it. As you do so you will find that your Stillness increases. Over time this Stillness goes into Emptiness and then things begin to really take off in the subtle dimension of the inner realm. As you approach nothingness the whole inner realm lights up and takes off, so to speak. Now you are more able to see the depth of your holding on to separateness and are able to embrace increasing wholeness. Wonder of wonders. Look how life has changed. And you look forward to every new moment, for in each you become more whole.

How does this play out in the external world of form. One that struck me was in John Cock's website where he mentions that Bultmann's commentary on the Gospel of John came to announce to the world at that time that the *Logos* was for and within everyone. Another item is from my Mentor's Mentor wherein he said "When God's love exploded the universe was created. All creation is but a pulsation of love." Love is Source...Love is Consciousness...Love is Life. Therefore our true nature is love. We are love, we live love and are fulfilled in love. True Love is all there is. We also hear in the dual commandments revealed in the Axial

Age in which Christianity coined, "Thou shall love the Lord thy God with all thy heart, soul, mind and strength, and thy neighbor as thyself." I often hear, in myself and others: "Well, how do I respond? Do I believe certain things, feel certain ways, commit myself or surrender to what is?" Try this: No matter what comes, recreate it in yourself exactly as it is, with gratitude and joy and live out of its fullness with love.

Love has become a whipping post for many in that we usually only know conditioned love. But when we experientially know unconditional love then all sorts of things light up anew. Love is compassion, kindness, forgiveness (no grudges or knee-jerk striking back), patient, long suffering, and non-judgmental. (Each of us can experientially add to this list.) Another simple but profound Axial Age gift is the Golden Rule. "Do unto others as you would have them do unto you."

One last remark: Do not let your new wisdom be such that you posses it in a separate way. It, like everything, is a gift of Grace. You are no closer or further from Life than everything else. Everyone's life, as well as all things, is sacred, and everyone's experience is valid for him or her. Each is unique with his/her particular experiences. Honor all; allow them to be who they are. They are sacred and live out their lives as best they see fit. I leave you with a gift I received from another. Always remember:

> "Love is not a need but an ecstasy.
>
> Neither a mouth thirsting, nor an empty hand outstretched forth.
>
> But rather a heart enflamed and a soul enhanced."

Remarks by John Silber

From his current home in Boston, Massachusetts.

In a note to me after my fifteenth year at Boston University, Jim Mathews cited a passage from the Talmud reflecting on the life of service: "You are not required to finish the task; neither are you permitted to lay it down." The rich legacy left to the Methodist Church by the brothers James and Joseph Mathews, like their lives of service, is something that will never be completed but will continue to be transformative as long as it is kept alive and never laid down.

Bishop James K. Mathews, as one would expect of a bishop, was a builder with a singular gift for bringing people together in working alliances and contributing sound advice and imaginative suggestions to any institution with which he had an affiliation. As a Trustee of Boston University, he exceeded all reasonable expectations of stewardship. When the University separated from its official control by the United Methodist Church by Trustees selected by that body, Bishop Mathews was asked to serve at the request of the new board. Such was Jim Mathews' service to the University as a Trustee that when he moved to Washington and was no longer our Bishop, the University continued to elect him to its Board of Trustees even though we had no ecclesiastical claims on his talents. Jim could have left Boston University with a friendly handshake and devoted himself to his different causes: the unification of Methodists worldwide, research on the faiths of India, the supervision of missionary councils. Instead, and despite demands on his time, he continued to serve our University for another 30 years.

Remarks by John Silber

Jim leveraged his influence and legacy by his inspired marriage to Dr. E. Stanley Jones's daughter Eunice. She was a partner in all his efforts. Without her, he could never have become a prolific writer of ten books and countless articles. They were both inspired by and dedicated to her father's causes of Christian evangelism and ecumenism. Their partnership took them throughout the globe in a series of adventures dedicated to these objectives.

Shortly after Jim's retirement, the council of bishops of the United Methodist Church commissioned him to write a book on the meaning of episcopacy in the tradition of John Wesley. This book was published with the title, Set Apart to Serve.

Bishop Mathews' courage and outspoken conviction resonated magnificently at Boston University, for we were an institution that had opened our doors to persons of all races and religions with our founding in 1869. There were blacks in the first student body of Boston University. I can't imagine any leader in the United Methodist Church who has contributed more to the ideals and principles on which the Church was founded and has been sustained than Bishop James K. Mathews.

He was ably assisted at a great distance by his brother Joseph, who was not one dedicated to bringing people together, but rather to waking them up. I met Joseph Mathews in Austin, Texas, in 1956. Although he was not a member of the faculty, he taught courses in what was called the Christian Faith and Life Community, courses that were as rigorous and intellectually demanding as any in the university. He was, as I once remarked, a spiritual Pied Piper who abhorred disciples but had eager followers. He attracted students who thirsted after the spiritual insight and the knowledge he offered. He recognized the centrality of existentialism at that time, the concern of young people to find answers to the question, "Who am I, and what am I here in this life to accomplish?" He didn't give them answers, but he guided them on the paths to explore while they attempted to answer these fundamental questions for themselves.

Joseph's hatred of idolatry was such that having accepted an invitation to preach before the First Baptist Church in Austin, he threw their huge pulpit Bible over his shoulder and onto the floor with a great noise. The congregation was shocked, but he calmly asked, "Do you worship this fetish? This idol? This book? Or are you prepared to go beyond that and find the message and guidance that this book has to offer? As a book, it's just another object. As a guide to our individual lives, it is of central importance. Its meaning, not its physicality, is central." Members of that Baptist congregation, mostly literalists, had to rethink their relationship to the book that they had elevated to the status of deity.

Joseph Mathews was one of the great prophets in the history of Methodism. His brother James was one of its most gifted missionaries, ambassadors and builders.

I felt personally the great impact of Joseph W. and James K. Mathews on my life. They were both guides and critics, but also supportive friends for whose lives I shall always be grateful. Their splendid work will never be forgotten by the United Methodist Church.

Our Legacy

These two original works from Joseph Wesley Mathews and James K. Mathews provide insight into the legacy that has been established by these two brothers.

The first is a 1973 paper now in the Archives of Joseph Wesley Mathews, Wesley Theological Seminary, Washington D.C.

The second is a sermon preached by Bishop James K. Mathews, now in possession of Anne Mathews-Younes in Potomac, Maryland.

Resurgement and the Religious[1]

Joseph Wesley Mathews, Chicago Illinois, Guardians Meeting – Chicago, April l3-l5, l973 Closing Plenary Address.

Grace be unto you and peace, from God our Father and our Lord Jesus Christ. Amen.

The glue of any movemental dynamic of the People of God is always an extremely fragile product. There are no temporal remunerations, finally. I believe that one of the crucial operating principles within our Order, for instance, is that among ourselves, we never thank anybody for anything. That is the way we honor one another. For how could you thank a man who has given his all for anything he does? So in the light of that principle, I have no thanks to give you; but I want you to know that I am grateful to God for what you have done in these last forty-four hours.

I believe an explosion is about to happen, and this time it will not be continental -- nor will it be international. It is very obvious that it will be global. This is not simply a geographical category. There has been no time in our history when we were any better prepared for a future event.

I believe that you can tell historical times by the rhythm of Justification and Sanctification. Those are theological categories. However, I am not using them in any particular theological frame of reference, but simply as shorthand symbols to point to discernable happenings in the dimension

---

The Global Guardians were a group of several hundred professionals from all walks of life, cultures and religious who worked hand-in-hand with the Institute staff to promote human development and service projects of EI/ICA worldwide.

of humanness itself. In theological circles, that which, in one frame of reference or another, is called "Justification," is the happening of *awakenment*. The suffix "ment" means "being" or "state of being." I like that -- *awakenment*: a state of being, a state of awakening or awakenness. For Sanctification, I like the word *resurgement*. It means "resurrection," to ride the new: "resurgence." I am interested in the dynamical state of the happening, the state of the happening of "resurgence," which is, to coin a word, "*resurgement*."

In the midst of the passing away of any age there are those who awaken; and the awakenment is always relative to profound insights into the raw deeps of humanness of what it means to be a human being. It is like the glorious cultures; not like a painting, a sculpture or a movie. Those are not inherently creative. They are simply a part of the manifestation of that creativity which is the culture. If you want to see raw sheer creativity, then you look at the great cultures of civilization -- gorgeous hunks of the manifest humanness that concern themselves for a moment with the mind of the Mystery beyond our comprehension and then fade away. In the midst of that very fading, it seems that mystery is all about us. Before the final mystery, these cultures pass away; and in the midst of their very passing the human happening of awakenment takes place -- *Lo here! Lo there! and Lo over there*! In that moment, awakenment has become almost a common reality, though it is never "common."

Man perceives today as one who has never perceived before. He always experiences that which no man has before ever perceived -- such new deeps of what it means to be a human being. Not only is culture being re-imaged and re-designed, but man himself, you and I, are being re-imaged and re-designed. What is happening now has never happened before. When it becomes somewhat common, then the dynamic of Sanctification takes place -- or "resurgence." And that is the beginning of the forging of the new. Of course, it began the moment that this one and that one awakened. Here again, mystery is all about us.

Do you not sense that that *new man* (I do not mean in a body, at the moment) is here? Yet he is not here. He has got to be called forth out of the marble that has been quarried. At this moment man expends his awakenment. This expending of awakenment is a happening of resurgement. Some never get beyond awakenment; and most, of course, never even personally experience awakenment.

At one time the Church used to cry over the people in the world who did not have the opportunity to experience awakenment. I suppose you would have to say that most people living today will have to go to their grave, as Ecclesiastes says, like cows that have never had the opportunity to experience the happening of awakenment. I believe, however, that many experience awakenment who perhaps do not experience the happening of resurgement. I am not certain here, but I believe it is true.

I want to deal indirectly with why that might be. At this moment in history it is a highly practical matter, only it is a happening you do not initiate. It is the expending of your awakenment, or giving concretion to your awakenment. It is the embodiment, in the civilizing process, of your awakenment. In one moment in history there is the reaching after meaning. In another moment in history meaning is poured into structures, or structures are forged to freight that meaning. This is the moment of resurgement -- as human a happening as awakenment.

Justification: The Awakenment Happening:

In the following diagram the bottom triangle is the analysis of awakenment which, of course, RS-I[1] deals with. It has nothing to do with doctrine or theoretic. It attempts to describe the phenomenological happening of awakenment. You begin in RS-I, down in the lower left-hand corner. I have used these categories of virtue or character qualities as a way to describe these quickly. In the left-hand corner is your God Lecture in RS-I.

Inescapable Contingency:

This is the happening in which suddenly you experience the last rug pulled out from under you. There you face the eternal irrationality

[1] RS-I: Religious Studies I, a 44 hour weekend course from the curriculum of the Ecumenical Institute, with sessions on God, The Christ Event, The Holy Spirit and the Church. Many of the authors of these papers refer to this course as part of their formative experience.

beyond your own capacity or any other man's capacity to reason. There is where you meet the Mystery. In the midst of the "no-thingedness" or nothingness is the first step of waking up as a human being. You die! You know nothing beyond that.

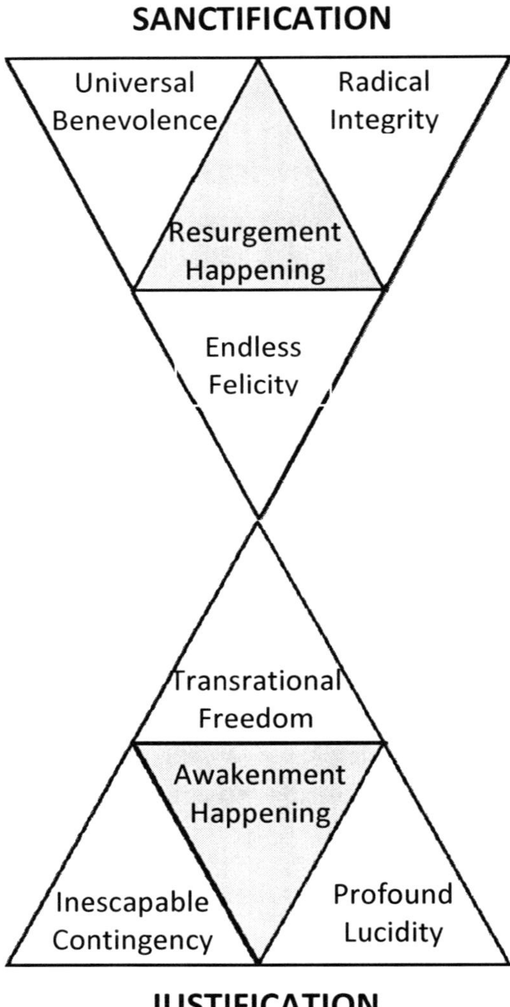

Profound Lucidity:

Yet lucidity, so profound that you cannot fathom it, comes in the midst of that experience. That is the Christ Lecture.

The final up-againstness you experience as Inescapable Contingency is not only an aspect of life -- *it is life*! In the Church we call that *the Word*! Either you accept your life of creaturehood, or you do not have any life. The one life you have is the very meaning of your life. I call that Profound Lucidity. I like that word "profound" these days. It means "radical," foundational, rudimentary, or fundamental. That is the Word: the painful, wonderful Word.

When it dawns on you that this is what life is all about, you are forced to make a decision. I use the word "forced" because you have no choice; you either have to choose the "no" or choose the "yes." If you choose the "no," then you blot out of your mind through one comforting escape or another the experience of Inescapable Contingency. You remain something less than a human being until the worms take over.

Transrational Freedom:

If you say "Yes," you discover what I call Transrational Freedom -- that you are in charge of the unbelievable gift of having one life to live and one death to die. You and you alone are in charge of it. There is no one to blame -- no wives, no children, no ancestors, and no external fates. That is the awakenment happening. It is not an idea about life; it is a happening. It is a happening of the deeps of life.

It is at this point that the resurgement happening can happen, and only at this point. When a man has his freedom -- that is, becomes his freedom, or takes upon himself the freedom he is -- he will discover that his freedom has to be spent. Kierkegaard said that if you have a penny and you spend it for a lollipop, you do not have a penny any more. You have got a lollipop. Freedom is like a penny; it has to be spent. The resurgement happening has to do with the authentic expenditure of the freedom that you are.

Sanctification: The Resurgement Happening

Universal Benevolence:

The resurgement happening begins equivalently at the top of the diagram, on the left hand where the virtue category is Universal

Benevolence. That happening only happens in the midst of the glee and the buoyancy of having grasped the "I am free!" All of life, in a strange, unbelievable way, has become good; it is your life. I like to walk on the beach in the mornings, I like the rain but I like sunny days, too. On some such day, or in some such series of circumstances while walking on the beach, the sun is shining and it is great to be alive, and then you stub your toe on a dead seagull. As if it had any *right* to intrude its death into this fantastic day of yours! Suddenly the sky falls in. It is not the dead bird. In one sense that had nothing to do with it, except that it was the occasion of the sky falling. The falling of the sky is what you mean by unlimited good will in which you become aware suddenly that you are responsible for the whole world.

It is not something intellectual -- it is just there. You are no longer responsible for your children. I cannot put the pain strongly enough. There is not such a thing anymore as your children. They do not exist anymore. There is no such a thing anymore as your nation. It does not exist anymore. You suddenly become aware that you are responsible for everything in creation (*all* the children, *all* the nations, *everything*). Schweitzer went to Africa to atone for the sins of the white man against the black man. He took them all on himself! You slowly become aware that you are responsible for everything that has ever happened. No longer is it, "I was not there!" "I did not do it!" It is just, "Yes, I am present." You are responsible for the whole future. That is not something intellectual. It is just there! It is an indicative! Your common law has no meaning anymore -- only the generations. You cry out, "That cannot be!" You know what I am talking about. You are crying it out now. A thousand-ton crane has dropped on you and driven you into the center of the earth. You try to roll this way and the burden rolls with you. You try to roll that way and it rolls with you. You are trapped! It is not that the inscrutable mystery has yanked the rug out from under you -- it has placed the world on top of you.

Radical Integrity:

Radical Integrity, profound integrity, has to do with being crushed by the weight of the world. It includes the awareness that this is what it means to be a man. I like the Jesus figure. John the Baptist baptized people for profound repentance; this turned upside down everything they have ever been taught. Jesus came to be baptized, and in the midst of that sign heard a voice, "Thou art my beloved son." That has to do with Radical Integrity. In the midst of this is the awareness that you did not first of all come out of a family; you did not first of all come out of a race; you did not first of all come out of a nation; you did not first of all come out of a church; you were, first of all, born of woman. You came out of humanity. A voice comes from deep within the cavernous dimensions of your being; the Word is screamed to you from the circumference of the universe itself: If this is what it means to be a man! My beloved son! This is what it is all about to be human – human consciousness.

For you, this is just the way it is. Everyone knows the Christ Lecture begins, "My spouse is the wrath of God in my life." When you are aware, the rug has not only been pulled out from under you but has been pulled out from under all that is, it is at that moment that profound lucidity happens. You hear the Word, "This is the way life is!" When I was younger and thinner, at this point in the lecture I would jump to one side to illustrate that you are thrown outside yourself; you are looking at yourself. Between you and yourself is an unbridgeable chasm, an abyss that you cannot get around. You cannot avoid it. You can only take it into yourself, and that is your freedom -- your Radical Integrity.

When the crash comes and you are thrown outside yourself, you become aware that this responsibility for everything is what it means to be human. There is an abyss; but instead of this abyss being an empty vacuum, it is brimming full of weakness. Some of my young colleagues tell me from time to time that I have grave self-doubt. I experience myself as being humiliated. Precisely when you grasp that weakness is what it means to be a man, then you grasp – you cannot deal with it. All of us great big men who thought we could handle the morality in this world, who thought we could handle the decencies of this world, who thought we could handle the normal demands of this world, we suddenly see ourselves as nothing other than sheer weakness. This is the ontological humiliation which is the core of consciousness itself. This is the way life is. "I am the light." Out of this is failure -- ontological failure.

If you succeed or if you do not succeed, it does not matter. You can be a little fish in a big pond, or a big fish in a little tiny pond. Now this is cut through, and you experience only failure. You discover that the abyss is filled with objectless pain. How can this be?

It is the happening of resurgement that has happened to you. Suddenly in the midst of life, without knowing why, your being is filled with a kind of pain. You never knew it existed. Someway you secretly know it is never going to go away. (Have I described the abyss enough for you?) You have just two choices! And you have to make the choice! It is either "no" or "yes." There is no deal you can make; you have gone too far.

If you say "no" then you turn into a malign or a benign zombie. For the rest of your life, if you are malign, you are mean. You do not know why, but you are mean. The women you know become mean, mean women. Some of you are married. The men are mean. You cannot see any reason why they are mean, they just are. You see what happens? This is why you pray that this resurgence does not happen to you. What goes away from you is what you learned in RS-I. It is wiped out of your memory. You no longer know your life is significant. You no longer know this world is good. It is taken away. So you are just mean, filled with hatred -- not hostility, but hatred. But you do not know what to direct your hatred at. Or if you are benign, you smile all the time. For the rest of your life you are just nice. If you want a pleasant domestic relationship instead of marriage, it will not be easy to find one. But people have forgotten why they are smiling. They just smile; nothing gets at them anymore.

Endless Felicity:

Or your answer is "Yes." This means, that the rest of your life you have to pay. You cannot really tell anybody about it. You just have to pay. When you return from the Center, the cloud of apostasy never goes away. You say "Yes" to it. You embrace it. That is who you are when you discover (using romantic poetry) a silver lining in the dark cloud. It is the silver lining in the dark cloud. The cloud never turns silver. It is then that you experience Endless Fulfillment. There is certitude in the midst of absolute uncertainty. It is always there. You know the struggle inside could not be there if it was not the way you will experience problemlessness.

> The peace that passes all human understancing happens exactly when you have every problem of the world upon your shoulders! You discover, right then, that you no longer have any problems.

In this moment of resurgence, Psychiatry will change. These arenas of life are not understood psychologically, but they have psychological effects. This is the moment when spontaneous joy of life breaks through an indescribable burden. This is when you grasp what every culture has always come up with -- the state of endlessness. The Greeks called it immortality -- the sense, even now, of participating in the beginning and the end of being itself. You have wanted fulfillment. I have just described this thing which you have yearned for all your life. I did not want to talk about this; but that is the happening of intentionally taking upon you this moment of resurgence in history. The Church has called that "Sanctification."

Becoming a Religious:

What I want to talk about is "Becoming a Religious." The happening in humanness that is the expenditure of your freedom, in which you decide your life in the midst of that happening, is what happiness and fulfillment are all about. In the midst of that happening, you discover you have a vocation for the first time in your life. You are elected, you are chosen. You become aware you are set aside. You become aware you are different from other people. God never calls the clergy. Culture calls clergymen and calls laymen. God only calls the Religious. God, or the Mystery in life, could not care less whether you are a Religious as a lay or as a cleric. The moment of resurgence and history is when society becomes aware of mysterious elections to be the Religious.

Many of you laymen in the room -- maybe not all of you clerics but some of you clerics -- have known for a long time that there is a strange thing here. I thought, until recently, that perhaps there was a difference between a religious cleric and a religious lay. Not so, a Religious is a man who knows what I am talking about. He has no question about his calling. He is called. The Religious is an engaged man. Whether in law, business, medicine, or priesthood, he is engaged to the bottom. No more time belongs to him -- all life is engagement. The Religious is a deeply disciplined man. He knows, he could not take three steps, otherwise. The Religious is a radically corporate man. He belongs to the whole race. No longer is there any sense of being an individual. He is corporate. The Religious is an obedient man. He is obedient with a strange kind of detachment that allows him to experience the Holy Spirit in his being as a power and a force most men would never dream of. Nobody can call a Religious or not call a Religious. He is already called; he is called to care about all of humanity. These things have to be done for him, for us.

In order to keep from being burned to a crisp, we first have to be given a context, in which this is related to the whole of history and not simply our own little interior being. Secondly, we have to be given a construct. If we try to do this alone, we are lost souls. That construct, I believe, has to be multifarious; but it has to be a construct. (I would like to talk about the way some of you are going to have to adjust your life for the rest of your days.) Lastly, it has to be given a climate. By a climate, I mean what I am doing now. Those of you for whom this has no meaning, forget that you are here for a while. I have been climatizing you. You have time over the next three years to work this through together. If I were you, I would read again The Journey to The East, or I would get a little book called The Journey of Kierkegaard. I believe that you should also read Dark Night of the Soul by St. John of the Cross, and even though I might understand only one out of every ten sentences, I would stay with it until I got to the bottom of it. That is what I mean by having a climate.

Who are you? Do any of you wish to accept yourselves? That is fine. That is what you ought to do. You are like an advisory board to what may be an unbelievable Global Movement. You understand that without such a board there could be no Global Movement. To be honest, sometimes I wish you were merely advisors. But you are not. You are what I have been talking about. You wonder what it means to be a man and launch out into the unknown like those who went before the mast for two years. You are before the Mast that would make any mast look ill. You are on the verge of adventure, and there are perils with adventure. I worry about you -- just a little.

Now, you have yourselves a good life till we meet again. Amen.

SERENDIPITY: A Sermon

at Metropolitan Memorial United Methodist Church

Bishop James K. Mathews, Washington DC – September 25, 2005

Texts: Exodus 17:1-7; Psalm 78: 1-4, 12-16; John 1:1-14; Philippians 2:5-11

GREETING: Grace be unto you and peace from God our father and our Lord Jesus Christ. And let me add: ***Mangwanani*** – that means "Sleep Well?" and it is the common greeting in Zimbabwe, from which Eunice and I have just returned from an assignment for the United Methodist Church. It is what one says in the morning when first encountering a neighbor or a companion and it implies the wish that one might have had a good night. And the proper response to this greeting is *Mangwanani*.... which in context means: "I did if you did!"

So that is my wish for you this morning, so I say to you *Mangwanani*....

We have been gone for some time, so this is something of a homecoming for me, so let me say what Metropolitan Memorial means to me. In one way or another, I have been related to this congregation, the National Church of United Methodism, for some 70 years.

Eunice and I first became acquainted with this congregation through an association with the American University across the street.

Then, in 1960 I was elected Bishop here by the delegates gathered at the Northeastern Jurisdiction of The Methodist Church.

When I was assigned as Bishop in 1972 to the National Capitol Episcopal Area, this congregation welcomed us back into your midst.

Serendipity: A Sermon

From my assignment as Episcopal leader in this Conference, I appointed pastors in this region for eight years, including the appointment of Dr. William A. Holmes to this very pulpit in 1974, where he subsequently served for 24 years.

After my retirement in 1980, and in between Episcopal assignments elsewhere, we -- Eunice and I -- very often worshipped here whenever we have been in town, and one of our daughters is actively associated with this congregation.

Now I am designated "Bishop-in-Residence" with this congregation – but I have yet to discover what tasks that entails... I often ask "What should I be doing?"

And, lastly, one day my funeral will be held here – for which I have already begun to make preparation.

I. For years I was a topical preacher. That is, I tried to address some issue of the day and then attempted to explore what light the Bible had to shed on it.

Then I became a lectionary preacher – and attempted to relate stated readings from the Old Testament, the Psalms, the Gospels, and the Epistles which have been chosen over a period of three years. This offers to the people an opportunity to survey virtually the whole Bible during each cycle. It also assures that the preacher is not carried away by his/her own favorite themes.

Lectionary preaching also has its drawbacks. Frequently I have noted that it is difficult to see how the four selections each Sunday relate to one another. Yet one must try.

Today's Old Testament lesson focuses on the Children of Israel during their exodus from Egypt. That story – of how slaves in Egypt were set free and molded into a nation – is told over and over again in the Scriptures and was for the Jews what the story of the Cross is to Christians. We recognize this even now as we are in the middle of what the Jewish community refers to as the "High, Holy Days." Just as in days of old, we as Christians are set free by the Cross – freed to serve God by the serving of others.

Specifically, we find the Israelites feeling abandoned in the desert – and without water.

"Give is water to drink," they cried to Moses. (That has a familiar enough ring to it these days!) Then the account states that Moses smote the rock with his staff and water gushed forth. That was that! But another question arose from the people: "Is the Lord among us or not?" The answer is a resounding "Yes!" and the story itself would not be told if this were not true. God is a refuge for his people – and this in the very hour of their need.

The Psalm for the day (Psalm 78), picks up the same theme. It recalls the mighty deeds of God for his people – deeds that they tended quickly to forget: God delivered them from bondage; God led them with a cloud by day and a fiery pillar by night; God divided the raging sea that they might pass through safely. (Does not the poetic imagery here still fire our imagination?)

Again, the Psalm refers to water gushing from the rock and quenching their parched throats. This cannot have been too different from helicopters in New Orleans delivering bottled water to those who agonized in thirst. These latter, of course, were not in a desert. There was "water, water everywhere, but not a drop to drink!" How often they, too, must have raised their voices: "Is the Lord with us or not?" "Does God care?" The answer is the same now as it was in days of old: "Yes!" a resounding "Yes!"

We next turn to the Epistle reading assigned for today.

If we give free range to our imaginations, we can perhaps picture ourselves as worshippers in an early Christian assembly in, say, a city like Antioch – where followers of Jesus were first called "Christians." Or perhaps, in Philippi, which apparently became the first church established in what we know today as Europe. A cantor lifts a hymn. You may follow it from the pew Bible before you if you wish, as I read it:

> "Let the same mind be in you that was in Christ Jesus,
>
> who, though he was in the form of God,
>
> did not regard equality with God

as something to be exploited,
but emptied himself, taking the form of a slave,
being born in human likeness.
And being found in human form,
He humbled himself
And became obedient to the point of death –
even death on a cross.
Therefore God also highly exalted him
and gave him the name
that is above every name,
So that at the name of Jesus,
every knee should bend,
in heaven and on earth and under the earth,
And every tongue should confess
that Jesus Christ is Lord,
to the glory of God the Father."

Philippians 2:5-11.

That's the Epistle for today – one of the most striking passages in the New Testament! These are perhaps the finest words St. Paul ever wrote. Here were followers of Jesus – scarcely fifteen years after the crucifixion – singing about and seeking the mind of Christ – longing to be like Jesus. A loftier view of Jesus has never since been formulated.

Long ago it happened that I preached my own ordination sermon, and this passage from Philippians was the exact text for that day. What exactly I said then, I cannot recall, but I was consumed then by those words even as I am now:

Jesus was like God…
But he emptied himself (the Greek term is *kenosis*)
He became a human being.
He humbled himself,
He became a lonely servant.
He suffered a slave's death – on a cross.
But then, God exalted him, lifted him up,
Restored him above all

The poetic imagery seems to suggest a kind of heavenly elevator service, if you will. There is a divine / human encounter. The Bible is full of this. Ours is a God-like Christ, and a Christ-like God. This is the very foundation of our confidence as Christians.

Do you recall Jacob's dream? In a desert place he tried to get a good night's sleep, using a rock for a pillow. It must have been a restless, tossing night. Jacob dreamed of a ladder stretched from earth to heaven, with angels ascending and descending. In his dream Jacob met God.

When he awoke, he said to himself, "Surely, the Lord is in this place and I did not know it…. How awesome is this place. This is none other than the house of God. This is the gate of heaven." Jacob called the place Beth-El, which means "the house of God."

It was, of course, a dream, a vision – yet whenever we sense the presence of God, we're at home, whether in a desert or a flood – we are at a gateway which may lead to a brand-new life!

Or recall the prophet Elijah (the very name means: "Yahweh-is-God"). He was snatched up to heaven in a whirlwind or a chariot of fire – much to the astonishment of the younger Elisha (whose name means: "Yahweh-is-salvation"). This, too, happened near Beth-el. This story should not seem so utterly strange, for in a jet-age, in which space travel is now common, a chariot of fire should not be too hard to imagine. The point is that, Biblically speaking, heaven and earth are linked. The horizontal and the vertical planes are related. The I-Thou and the I-Neighbor are joined at the hip. This Philippian hymn hints at the most basic Christian teaching: the Incarnation – which is how we speak of God sharing human experience.

The Gospel lesson from Chapter 1 of John is even more explicit: "The Word became flesh and pitched his tent among us." Our Creator has honored human beings by becoming one of us. Our calling, then, is to be fully human as Jesus was. This should give us hope when all else seems hopeless – even in the midst of a desert or storm. "Even there, love can be found, and where there is love, there is God" and God is love. God cares about what we have to go through.

II. I know I am supposed to be speaking of Serendipity. That's the title I myself chose for this sermon, after all. In a sense I have been talking of nothing else. For some, this may be a strange word. It is relatively new to the English language. It was coined by an English writer two hundred and fifty years ago, Horatio Walpole, in a book titled: <u>Three Princes from Serendip</u>.

You will not believe this, but I sometimes go two or three days without actually using this word. It means, "the faculty of finding surprising or desirable ends by accident." It came quickly to my mind after the massive tidal wave (or tsunami) which visited the Indian Ocean region after Christmas at the end of last year. Ceylon (now called Sri Lanka) was particularly hard-hit. Its old (Westernized) name was *Serendip*, from which serendipity is derived.

Each passing day after that tragic occurrence, the mounting toll spiraled until more than one hundred thousand people lost their lives and often all of their possessions, too.

Then there came almost immediately a world-wide out-pouring of help and concern. It was an unprecedented response and virtually universal in scope. The whole world had discovered the poor and suffering in a part of the globe that is easily forgotten by those of us in the West. Suddenly humanity became one family – which had been true all along. This is *serendipity*: goodness arising out of disaster.

III. We turn now to the present day and the present hour. What a time ours is: Two wars – the threat of avian flu – inflated gasoline prices. Just a month ago a former Secretary of the Navy declared that our country seemed to be more divided than ever before in his lifetime. We have been visited by a series of hurricanes, climaxing now in Katrina and threatened by Rita. In the midst of all this we watched the Senate hearings on a Supreme Court nomination – and on and on.

One need not try to put into words what we all have for days seen with our eyes on TV: what our people have suffered in these natural disasters. To contemplate all this is surely heartbreak to all except the most callous.

Yet if there has been bad news, there is also some good news. Once again, there has been an eruption of sharing: on a worldwide scale… and this time America is on the receiving end. "It is more blessed to give than to receive." This we are learning anew – and it is also probably more difficult to receive than to give.

The gifts flowed in from everywhere: from our nearest neighbors in Canada and Mexico; an offer of medical aid from Cuba; a gift of $1,000,000 from Bangladesh of all places, once characterized as the "basket case" of all nations; $5,000,000 from India; $40,000,000 from South Korea; aid from several countries in the Middle East; water purifiers from Sweden; communications equipment from Germany; help from Vietnam and even from North Korea! I just discovered a report that Africa University sent 15,000 sheets and pillowcases! This is a part of a long list of donors.

My eyes swell with tears as I write these words. Do we need further evidence of our common humanity? Of all the world's people, we Americans can now say, "We're family." <u>This</u> is *serendipity* – an unexpected blessing.

There was, of course, delay in proffering assistance, but it was due in large measure to our surprise at the magnitude of the need. Who can forget the makeshift signs from rooftops calling for HELP? Of course, the meaner side of human nature also showed itself. There was violence and looting – though it must be said this stemmed more from despair than anything else.

It is a ready human trait to engage in finger-pointing; in playing the "blame game." But note: African tribesmen long ago observed that when we point one finger at another, we point three fingers at ourselves. Nevertheless, some have blamed the mayor of New Orleans, the

Governor of Louisiana, the United States military, and, of course, the President – not to mention God! Not infrequently, human beings have not used their God-given wisdom when building our places of habitation. One would think we should, with prudence, avoid places unduly threatened by forces of nature. God can hardly be blamed for that.

Others confidently assure us that this disaster is God's vengeance -- for the world's insistence on Israel's withdrawal from Gaza; for our national rebellion against God; for abortion, homosexuality, feminism, and liberalism in general. I wonder how some claim to know so confidently the will of God, directing wrath against anyone who does not display the spirit of Christ? As though placing blame mirrors the spirit of Christ!

Apportioning blame is as futile as it is mean-spirited. President Bush has now accepted responsibility and accountability for the inadequate national response to the disaster. Our collective energies are now better devoted to the cure and recovery rather than continuing to play the blame game.

Thank God, the reality is that multitudes within the affected area, and outside it as well, have been engaged in humanity's proper business: <u>simply being humane</u>:

— they have opened their hearts

— they have opened their homes (after all, hospitality is a primary Christian virtue)

— they have opened their schools and colleges to displaced students

The full story of individual heroism and compassion can never be told. As a result of all this, we have questions before us that we often ignore.

As a result of this disaster, <u>we have rediscovered the poor</u>. Oh, we've noticed them before -- but they so easily slip from our minds when we are shopping in the malls. The fact is, we are told, that by sharing less than 1% of our national income, we could, by joining other rich nations, eliminate abysmal poverty from our world. Of course, there are some who say poverty is good for building character – but this is usually a view held by those who have never tried it.

We have rediscovered the residual racism which plagues our society. Can we not determine that, once and for all, we will overcome this scourge in our nation?

We have re-discovered the imbalance of medical access – on the whole our doctors, nurses and paramedics have acquitted themselves well in this battle zone of treatment and recovery. But – can we not devise ways that our great medical skills shall be made available to all before such a disaster, and in the normal course of daily life?

Is it not possible that while addressing the enemies outside our borders, we could give more attention to the enemies within – our greed, our hubris, our excessive national pride? We have reason to seek humility. We are one nation under God – whether or not we insert that phrase into our Pledge of Allegiance! If we accept this, what does that mean in our attitudes and the way we live our lives?

Is it possible – just possible – that we can use this national tragedy to fuel a new drive to overcome our pettiness and move toward a more full unity as a people?

Who am I to speak of taxation? But I do believe that as citizens we should accept a fuller tax burden, to rebuild the damaged parts of our country and not impose this burden on later generations. Rather than more tax refunds for the rich, ought we not pay down the national debt as was happening in the late 1990s under the previous administration? This would mean that rather than paying interest annually on a rising debt, we might reach a place where we could provide a permanent tax cut to all, including those at the bottom of the ladder.

Can we not see taxation as the dues we pay for the privilege of living in a free society? Can we not all lift a part of the burden resting on those who have suffered from floods by sharing a measure of their loss? To do so, we might discover that the playing field might indeed be leveled.

During recent days we have had a National Civics Lesson. It has come through the Senate hearings for a new Chief Justice of the Supreme Court. We have been reminded anew of the wise and essential balance of power that our Constitution provides – its checks and balances. We have been schooled afresh about the rule of law. We have heard the summons once again of liberty and justice for all.

We know that ours is an unfinished democracy. The *Preamble* to the Constitution that we learned as school children has yet to be fulfilled.

> "We, the People of the United states, in Order to form a more perfect Union, establish Justice, insure domestic Tranquility, provide for the common defense, promote the general Welfare, and secure the Blessings of Liberty to ourselves and our Posterity, do ordain and establish this Constitution for the United States of America."

This states our national Goals! Shall we not pursue them?

May we not believe that in our day we can have a new birth of freedom and be a city set upon a hill – for **all** the world to see?

We who have had our spirits renewed and our consciences enlivened by the Gospel are the very people who are assigned this duty.

Amen.

Our Challenges

The following addresses look through the legacy and discuss the challenges before People of Spirit in the 21st Century. Each of the authors, of course, brings their own perspective on their previous involvement with the Mathews brothers, and highlights the influence that these brothers manifest in their own lives. Many additional workshop addresses also further illuminate the transformation of this legacy into practical engagement in the world today. The material from the workshops will be published in the subsequent Volume II and be made available on the website: www.resurgencepublishing.com.

Opening Address

The Mathews Brothers:

Great Mission Leaders of the 20th Century Who Challenge 21st Century Mission Leaders to be Holistic, Culturally Competent and Inquisitive

John R. Schol, United Methodist Bishop of the National Capital Area

Welcome to Washington, D.C. and the symposium to honor the ministry of Bishop James and Dean Joseph Mathews, Transforming the Legacy – People of Spirit in the 21st Century. We are grateful for the leadership of Rev. Maynard Moore who worked tirelessly to bring us together for this important symposium. His visionary mind and steadfast persistence created the opportunity for us to learn, grow and recommit to the ministry of theological and social engagement. Maynard, we thank you.

We are also indebted to Wesley Theological Seminary, an innovative and forward-thinking institution that is developing spiritual leaders that will transform the Church, communities and the world. The seminary is exposing spiritual leaders to the richness of the biblical story and church tradition so that spiritual leaders make and engage disciples in ministries of hope and justice around the world. Wesley Seminary's latest innovation, Wesley at Mt. Vernon Place, will put students in the heart of the city where faith, society and public policy all intersect. This new center, which houses and equips students for spiritual leadership, halfway between the White House and the Capital, will narrow the distance between the institutions that are called to serve and the Gospel challenge to preach good news to the poor, proclaim release to the captives, the recovery of sight for the blind and to proclaim the Lord's favor. Wesley is a bridge between

- biblical scholarship and biblical living,
- church history and present day disciple making,
- ethical teachings and justice for all God's people,
- theological thinking and heart-filled caring - living with the poor, the homeless and those searching for hope and salvation.

We are blessed to have such a fine seminary in our area.

Today we are also grateful to Wesley for creating a permanent archive for the writings and work of Dean Joseph Wesley Mathews where researchers and students may be inspired by the life and work of Rev. Mathews. Joseph W. Mathews is synonymous with the Ecumenical Institute, today known as the Institute of Cultural Affairs. In the words of Stuart Umpleby:

> In 1954 the World Council of Churches met in Evanston, Illinois, where a resolution was passed to begin a center for the training of lay people in North America, taking as an example the Ecumenical Institute of Bossey, Switzerland. Around the same time a group of faculty members and students at the University of Texas began to study the relationship between their faith and contemporary life. Rev. Joseph Mathews and others created a curriculum for students and laity. The community began to work on the role of churches and congregations in society. In 1962, Joe Mathews was appointed dean of the Ecumenical Institute in Chicago. He brought with him a group of people, seven families, who had been experimenting with a disciplined life of worship, study, and service, the Acts 2 community in which they shared all things in common and gave to any who had need.[1]

[1] Stuart A. Umpleby, The George Washington University, "A Global Strategy for Human Development: The Work of the Institute of Cultural Affairs", with Alisa Oyler, Published by ICA International, 2009.

These seven families, forming a community in Evanston, Ill., primarily focused on church renewal. It was their move to an urban neighborhood on the West Side of Chicago in 1963 that engaged them in developing a holistic community, which included economic development. This work became known as "Fifth City" and used door-to-door organizing to politically engage communities to bring about community renewal.

In addition to door-to-door organizing they used what came to be known as Focused Conversation, a way of thoroughly discussing a subject, delving deep into factual, emotional, rational, and action-oriented components in a natural sequence.

> Cultural Development also became pivotal to the thinking and activities of the Ecumenical Institute through a social process triangle – of political, economic, and cultural systems. The purpose of the triangle was to emphasize the importance of culture in development, an aspect of the social process that tended to be neglected. The Ecumenical Institute was always concerned with the entire social process, but they felt that culture was a key component. (Umpleby/Oyler)

Their mission spread globally as they sought to demonstrate comprehensive village development. The village development worked holistically, dealing with economic, social and cultural programs, addressing all the problems in the village and involving all the village's people.

While Joe Mathews was creating community in Chicago and around the world, his brother, Bishop James K. Mathews was also making a difference as a world mission leader. His work through the Board of Missions, now known as the General Board of Global Ministries, was reaching new generations of disciples, starting new churches and addressing pressing human needs found in communities. His work took him to many different countries, particularly to India where he fell in love with the country, its people, and with Eunice Jones. He married Eunice and together they worked passionately with the people of India and other countries where they proclaimed good news to the poor, release of the captives, recovery of sight to the blind and the favor of the Lord.

The Mathews Brothers

One of my first experiences with Bishop James K. Mathews was in a small boutique hotel in New Jersey shortly after my consecration as a bishop. The Northeastern Jurisdiction College of Bishops, including retired, active and newly consecrated bishops, were there to orient the new bishops. While checking out of the hotel, Bishop Mathews engaged a couple from India in their native tongue. I wondered who is this man who speaks in several different languages and with such wisdom.

Bishop Mathews has been a man who possesses wisdom beyond his years and there have been a lot of years (Bishop Mathews is well into his nineties). He had an ability to focus on the matters before him and to look outward to the possibilities of what could be. He pioneered mission for the church, opened opportunities for women and African Americans, and used the teaching office of the episcopacy to shape and inspire the church.

In my brief tenure as a bishop, I witnessed at Council and College of Bishops' meetings that when Bishop Mathews stood to speak, people became expectant and ready to receive a word of wisdom and insight. In his retirement he was used to lead several conferences, including Zimbabwe, during times of important transition.

The lives of the Mathews brothers were rivers that flowed from the same pool of water - family values, faith, strong educational experiences and engagement in the world. While the rivers of their life took them to different experience of ministry, the flow of their lives continued toward a common destination of making the Kingdom of God a reality in their time. They had common principles that guided them:

- development of the whole person,
- cultural competence, and
- an inquisitive mind.

These same principles are building blocks for the future mission of the church.

Holistic Development:

Holistic development is paradoxical. On the one hand human and community development must be broad and encompass the many facets of a community or a person's experience. On the other hand, mission that is life-changing and sustainable, must be specifically focused. As a denomination, United Methodists learned this through the Community of Shalom initiative. Shalom demonstrated that community transformation requires integrated strategies and focused attention on systemic change through community development. The biblical Shalom Community sought to integrate five strategic areas:

- health and healing,
- prosperity through economic development,
- strengthening multicultural relationships,
- spiritual renewal, and
- care for the environment.

Communities that experience poverty and decline need a holistic approach rather than addressing an individual need in isolation.

On the other hand, a holistic approach must focus its efforts in a concentrated area so that resources and success build on each other. In the Community of Shalom initiative, urban communities focused on a several block area, rather than the entire community. Developing a portion of the community was a way of making small victories become large victories. Directed strategies in a defined area created broad change across the community. In other words, by focusing, change occurred and began to be replicated in other parts of the community. It is the principle of the Ecumenical Institute's Fifth City movement of beginning in a portion of a section of Chicago's West Side and developing the "village" holistically.

This requires collaboration with not only other church partners, but civic and business partners as well. This is the Mount Vernon Place strategy in which churches and seminary partner with other organizations to create a zone of ministry that rebuilds people and community. It is the principle of the No Malaria campaign in which the church, the Gates Foundation, the NBA, Orkin Pest Control Services, and a host of other organizations work together to end Malaria one community at a time. Ridding communities of disease restores not only health and healing but economic renewal and revival of the spirit.

The future of mission is holistic yet focused in specific areas to demonstrate and build on renewal.

Cultural Competence:

Thomas Freidman in his book, The World is Flat, spoke of a world in which a McDonald's drive-through order in an urban center was taken by an individual working from home in rural Midwestern community who sent the order via the Internet back to the store's workers. Many of us have had this experience when calling for on-line assistance to a help desk in India for our computer that is made in China by a company headquartered in California. The great global divide has been narrowed by technology. But this does not mean we are competent in navigating various cultural differences.

While serving as the United Methodist urban staff person at the General Board of Global Ministries in the mid-1990s, I remembered a debate about starting a Korean Mission Conference in the United States. Hae Jong Kim, bishop of the New York West Area at the time, made a passionate plea for a conference such as this to have the ability to recruit and deploy Korean pastors and develop Korean United Methodist spiritual leaders to start new Korean congregations. A group of Korean female pastors argued vehemently against the proposal because it might mean that they would not receive a pastoral appointment in a Korean United Methodist congregation because of the cultural values of Korean male clergy. The directors of the General Board of Global Ministries defeated the proposal. Former Bishop Kim said to the directors after the vote, "you are right and I am right".

He was correct. The spread of the Korean Church in the United Methodist Church is best done by a group of people who are Korean. And the directors of GBGM were also right.

The questions facing us today include what does a child of African-American and Korean parents serve for dinner to their gay Hispanic neighbor? And the issue is not cultural food, but the fact that the neighbor is a vegan. Cultural competence is about navigating the ever-changing culture with authenticity and transparency open to new understanding and experiences. As cultural expert Erik Law teaches, it is knowing yourself and your own culture before trying to understand and be understood by another culture. It is knowing your own resources and gifts through your cultural heritage and how they are your gifts and not necessarily the gifts for others.

Culturally competent mission is acknowledging and building on the gifts and assets of the people where the mission is being lived out.

Inquisitive Mind:

When I meet with Bishop Mathews, he wants to know what I am up to and what is happening, not only in the Baltimore-Washington Conference, but around the world. He has an inquisitive mind. One of the reasons the church has lost its power to transform is because it lost its inquisitiveness. It stopped asking good questions and instead became the dispenser of answers. It stopped learning about current and future realities and asking "what if" but instead lived out of what it knew and the answers it had. Reading, learning, listening and wondering are the keys to future mission. As Joe Mathews taught, we must look at an issue through factual, emotional, rational, and action-oriented questions exploring the cultural, developmental and educational aspects of mission.

Once while working with a group of church and community leaders in the Kensington section of Philadelphia, I asked, what are the assets of this community? I felt embarrassed asking the question. After all, the church we were sitting in had a leaky roof, outside its doors were young people selling and using crack, the church sat on a corner of a block that looked like bombed-out Iraq with boarded up and dilapidated homes in a community where all the businesses, banks, supermarkets, corner delis had all left town. Assets? I was afraid they would send me packing. But we always began helping churches start a Community of Shalom by asking, "tell us about the assets of this church and community." I received an education. The group came up with two pages of assets. These assets became the building blocks for starting a new worship service, a new business and an effort to renew the spirit of the people and the community. Through a process of inquisitiveness, of inquiry, a group of people felt empowered to be mission.

So today we ask for the future mission of the church, where is the inquisitiveness of the church that proclaims the Gospel through holistic development and cultural competence? That is a question which, perhaps, you can help us answer.

Reference cited:

Umpleby, Stuart A, and Alisa Oyler, A Global Strategy For Human Development: The Work of the Institute of Cultural Affairs, December 8, 2009, http://www.ica-international.org/history_2.htm.

Keynote Address

Two Brothers, One Mission: To Build the Earth

Rev. Dr. William A. Holmes, Baltimore-Washington Conference (retired)

Twenty years after Albert Camus participated in the French underground resistance during World War II, and after he won the Nobel Prize for Literature, he wrote in Resistance, Rebellion, and Death, the following challenge: (p. 71)

> What the world expects of Christians is that Christians should speak out loud and clear ... The grouping we need is a grouping of men [and women] resolved to speak out clearly and pay up personally. ...We are still waiting, and I am waiting, for a grouping of those who refuse to be dogs and are resolved to pay the price that must be paid so that a man [human being] can be something more than a dog.

The words of that challenge reverberate through the intervening decades and have dangerous implications for this Symposium. During these next few days, we just might do something to alter the trajectory of history in our own time – even if it's only by one-one thousandth of a degree. We will have, at least, bent a little history. Or, during these next few days, we just might do nothing but venerate the Mathews brothers. We Christians excel at veneration and we couldn't have two more worthy subjects.

BUT: have you noticed: The planners of this Symposium have set up a fire-wall against vacuous tributes to the Mathews? The name of the fire-wall is "Workshop Tracks:" breakout groups where we will literally refine visions into specific goals, goals into strategies, strategies into time-lines, and time-lines into accountability. It's as though they hung a sign on the front door saying "No abstractions allowed."

The planners of this Symposium are hoping -- they are requesting -- they are demanding that we go beyond tributes to Jim and Joe, and shove out into the world to radically reclaim it for God's sake – which is for the sake of the humanizing, civilizing process. And, not incidentally, this is precisely what it might mean to "honor the work" of Bishop Jim and Brother Joe, two men who, in their day, "spoke out clearly," "paid up personally," and changed the course of history for thousands, hundreds of thousands, if not millions, of lives – including my own.

Since my earliest seminary days I've been a camp follower of the Mathews' juggernaut. Seldom have I been on the inside, but never so far away on the outside that I could ignore the claim these two men laid upon my life. Initially, I experienced that claim many years ago. Now, I'm an eighty-year-old United Methodist minister in my 12th year of retirement. I'm "deaf as a post," have a balance problem, walk like I'm "three sheets to the wind," and steady myself with a $10 cane from Mexico. In my more sober moments I ask myself, "What in the hell am I doing *here*, and when do I get to retire from *this*?" (despite the fact I already know the answer to both questions.) So, I'm still a camp follower.

My assignment this morning is to give the Keynote Address divided into two parts. In the first part, I'm to talk about the "enduring truths" of the Mathews' legacy, and in the second part, I'm to locate where some of those truths are being applied in our own time. In both instances, I simply hope to stir your own brooding about and contribution to this subject.

As to enduring truths, I will briefly mention four, how these truths were incarnated in the life of each of the brothers, and through them, to the lives of others. And, with the risk of being self-referential, after much deliberation, I've decided to include a word about how each of these men first intersected my own life. I do this, knowing full well, given the opportunity, most of you in this Symposium could offer comparable accounts.

Enduring Truths

1. *To be in Christ is to have one, primary, vocation*: *"To renew the church for the sake of renewing the world."* I hope you marked that entire sentence. It's not "to renew the church" – period. It's "to renew the church *for the sake of* renewing the world." What that really means is having two vocations. There is what Bother Joe called your "para-vocation," the one alongside your primary vocation. Your para-vocation is the one that pays your salary or pension, and puts bread on the table. But your primary vocation is packed like a stick of dynamite into one little word: the word is *care*. Not to care casually, but to care radically, profoundly, sacrificially for others. Thereby, you might find yourself *renewing the church for the sake of renewing the world.*

2. *We are always on duty.* Bishop Jim writes in A Global Odyssey, "being a Christian is life-long and world-wide; ... we are always under a life sentence." Brother Joe used to say: "You get to retire when you reach the age of 90 – unless you live to be 91!" And Felton May has always said "I don't intend to rust out. I intend to burn out!" Felton's been retired now almost as long as I have, but when you heard him speak last night, there can be no doubt but that he's still burning! *We are always on duty.*

3. *The Double Paradox: You give your life in order to find it, and, you engage the particular to address the universal.* Neither of these paradoxes makes any sense in the usual meaning of "sense." They couldn't be more counter-intuitive. The logic of the world is that you don't give something away – especially your own dear life – if you cherish it. Rather, you seize, grasp, and hold on to what you value with all your might. Giving something away is called "losing:" a vessel being poured out is being "emptied." How could you possibly lose your life and pour it out in a way that would give meaning to your existence?

And as far as addressing universal crises – where do you begin? Poverty is rampant, starvation is in ascendancy, new and old illnesses and diseases mock human efforts, wars and rumors of wars define more and more societies – most especially this one. The number of crises in our time is exponential and overwhelming. How naive, how Pollyanna to presume that any group of persons could even begin to "fix" the world. Come on! And yet ... And yet the secret of the double paradox – the best kept secret in the world – continues to be passed from one generation to the next. A strange "community of possibility" exists in history to model the "divine foolishness": *You give your life in order to find it, and, you engage the particular to address the universal.*

4. *The church has been renewed.* Toward the end of the 1950s, the theoretical task of church renewal had been accomplished. What has been emerging since is operating images and scouting expeditions to demonstrate what it means to care in the family, the community, the nation and the world. Even though this is the "long march," worldwide and history long, we are not charismatic revolutionaries. We are structural revolutionaries, revolutionaries with a plan. And, undergirding it all is a "spirit training" of "serious fun" which includes singing, dancing, waltzing and grand balls. While giving our lives, we have the time of our lives! *The Church has been renewed*; now we're "mopping up."

How were these four truths concretized in the lives of Bishop Jim and Brother Joe, and through them, transmitted to the lives of others? I begin with Brother Joe because he was the first of the brothers to confront me with the radical implications of what it means to "be in Christ."

As a freshman in Seminary, on my first day, I sat in a classroom full of first year students waiting for the arrival of the controversial Professor Joseph Wesley Mathews – of whom we had all heard, but hardly knew what to expect. Eventually, he arrived and stood at the front of the room in a long silence – looking each one of us over. Finally, he spoke: "Before you came through that door," he said, "I knew more about each one of you than you would want your mother to know." Truth be told, he didn't know "squat" about any of us. But Joe Mathews knew himself. He knew the demons with which he struggled in the deeps of his own consciousness were not all that different from the demons that stalk the consciousness of every other human being. He then proceeded to talk, not only about himself, but about all the rest of us as well, and how the Gospel, with its radical implications, was meant for every person in that room. We were addressed, and *from that day on*, I listened and reconsidered what my life was really all about.

After a while, Brother Joe had an opportunity to work in a venue larger than a denominational seminary. He left Perkins School of Theology to become the Dean of Curriculum for the Christian Faith and Life Community in Austin, Texas. After traveling the world to learn of various religious orders, he returned to Austin to form a disciplined, religious cadre which eventually became the *Order: Ecumenical*. During this time, Religious Studies I (RS-I) was created; pedagogues were trained, and RS-I began to spread throughout the Southwest, then the nation, and finally the world.

Then came the move to Chicago with the complete renewal and reconstruction of a ghetto on the West side which became known as Fifth City – the mother-model replicated in the twenty-four time zones of the world. The *Order: Ecumenical* created Religious Houses in Los Angeles, Boston, Chicago, Atlanta, and eventually the Order morphed into the Institute for Cultural Affairs (ICA).

At the time of Joe's death in 1977, the ICA was established in 47 countries, and operated through an international community of families consisting of over 2,000 persons bonded in an experimental secular-religious order. This order has also been the core of a movement of over 100,000 colleagues across the world. By 1982, over 50 International Training Institutes for laity and clergy had graduated a new generation of ecumenical church leadership in Latin America, Africa, Asia, India, Australia and Europe. These leaders have been the catalysts for an explosion of self-help Human Development Projects in 43 nations. Meanwhile, the Chicago ICA staff has operated the International Conference Center and Community Resource Center serving over 1,000 clients per week as the largest one-stop social center in the nation. The "long march" of renewing the world has begun.

As for Bishop Jim, incarnating these values meant advancing the renewal of the church from *within* the institution, and he didn't hesitate to use the appointment process to that end. That's how he turned my life, and the life of my family, inside out and upside down at a time when we were assiduously content. Having spent half of my 46 years of ministry in the state of Texas, I finally found myself serving the church I had always dreamed of serving: University Methodist Church in Austin. The University of Texas, at that time, had 40,000 students. The church was strategically located on the edge of the campus, the congregation was "town and gown," and my six years in that community were everything I'd ever hoped for. Nancy, as State Vice President of the League of Women Voters, headed up the League's lobbying corps at the state capitol. Both our sons were stars on the high school basketball team, with one of them graduating and heading for a Texas college, and the other poised for a glorious high school senior year. Only in my mid-forties, I was already fantasizing about finishing my ministry right there, and retiring in Shangri-la.

Then came the phone call from Bishop Jim; It was not a mandate. He didn't try and overwhelm me with his "Episcopal authority." He issued an invitation, an opportunity that I interpreted as a claim I could not ignore. He talked about his "missional vision" for the national church of our denomination, a church located across from the campus of The American University, and attended by a number of U.S. Senators, Congressmen, and a soon-to-become-a-congregation-member, Associate Justice of the Supreme Court, Harry A. Blackmun. Most of all, he talked about the potential power of the church's pulpit, and what it could mean for a preacher to lobby for the Gospel from that pulpit, crying, "Thus saith the Lord!"

After a family conference, the four of us decided to set out on a new adventure. We moved to Washington, D.C., and for the next 24 years I preached from that pulpit, trained pedagogues, and conducted RS-I retreats three or four times a year for members of the congregation and other churches – all because Bishop Jim defined the appointment process in terms of a compelling mission.

At the same time, however, the Bishop never hesitated to creatively exploit opportunities *outside* the church to influence secular power. He took full advantage of consultations with Prime Minister Indira Gandhi of India, and with Presidents John F. Kennedy, George H. W. Bush, William Jefferson Clinton, Associate Supreme Court Justice Harry A. Blackmun, and a number of other national and world figures. His vision was always global, but his *praxis* was always local, whether applied in settings secular or ecclesiastical.

On Easter Sunday, 1964, he and Bishop Charles F. Golden – one of Methodism's first African American Bishops – attempted to worship and thereby integrate Galloway Memorial Methodist Church in Jackson, Mississippi. But they were turned away. This denial of access to Methodist Bishops seeking to celebrate the Resurrection on Easter ricocheted throughout the denomination, and considerably advanced the cause of civil and religious rights.

In each of the Episcopal areas that he served, Bishop Jim instituted "Study Days" for all his clergy, and did the teaching himself. While presiding over the greater Washington area, through the appointment process, he considerably advanced the cause of inclusiveness for African Americans, women, and various racial minorities. In 1978, Native Americans dramatized their plight by participating in what they called "The Longest Walk," starting in California and ending in Washington D.C. Bishop Jim not only welcomed them and joined them in their walk into the nation's capital, he arranged for them to stay in our churches, raised $75,000 toward their walk, and interceded for them with the FBI and the National Parks Service to allow the pitching of tepees on the Mall.

While in Washington, he agreed to chair the Board of Trustees at The American University; organized the InterFaith Conference of Metropolitan Washington which is today, the most widely representative body of different faiths in the United States; and he instituted the Churches' Center for Theology and Public Policy with its innumerable contributions to some of the church's most prophetic actions – including the Council of Bishops' 1985 document, <u>In Defense of Creation</u>, backing nuclear arms control. The list stretches far beyond the time allotted for this presentation, but suffice it to say that, although the *Discipline* of the denomination required Bishop Jim to officially retire at a certain age, the Council of Bishops called him out of that retirement time and again. He has the distinction of having served more Episcopal appointments than any other bishop in the 230 years of United Methodism. Bishop James K.

Mathews is the personification of mission "world-wide and history-long," – a mission which has always been for him a willing "life sentence."

The Claim of the Mathews' Legacy in Our Time

(with examples of where "Building the Earth" is happening today)

Since I can't "channel" either of the brothers, this is my own, subjective list of renewal efforts – some secular, some ecclesiastical, and some a little of both -- including, I must add, organizations to which I've been introduced by members of my own family. And, as before, I'm certain that most of you, given the chance, could offer comparable accounts.

On the semi-secular side, I state the obvious by affirming how International Training Institutes and Human Development Projects are succeeding in renewing the world. Although having never directly participated in these efforts, I know the evidence is overwhelming that they continue to provide some of the most comprehensive and compelling models for renewing the world.

Another semi-secular project in which I have participated is the Industrial Areas Foundation (IAF), founded in 1942 by Saul Alinsky. At the time of his death in 1972, the national staff of community organizers at IAF observed that each of them was a member of a religious community. Consequently, they set about building a new IAF around organizing Protestants, Roman Catholics and Jews into political action networks. Presently there are 59 IAF affiliates in 21 states, Canada, the United Kingdom, Germany and South Africa. Each affiliate chooses it own acronym as its nomenclature, builds trust between people of different congregations, sets its own politically "winnable" goals, and eventually holds large, ecumenical rallies with elected officials in attendance and eager to hear proposals from the very constituents who elect them.

In the greater Washington/Baltimore area, four IAF affiliates considerably advance the civilizing process. There's WIN (the Washington Interfaith Network) launched by a number of us as DC pastors; there's AIM (Action in Montgomery) which my son, Will, helped organize on behalf of affordable housing and other goals; there's PATH (People Acting Together in Howard), another county-wide organization; and BUILD (Baltimoreans

United for Leadership Development). IAF is "bending history." It is one of many semi-secular change-agents.

Then, there are those change-agents in which members of my own family have instructed me. There's Habitat for Humanity, in which we have a granddaughter serving on the Habitat staff in Americus, Georgia, and presently planning for our whole family to travel, next July, to build Habitat houses in Cameroon, Africa, where – not incidentally – we have another granddaughter serving in the Peace Corps. (Parenthetically, I should say these two granddaughters are sisters, and have a younger sister still in college. When you ask her about her plans when she graduates, she says: "I'm marrying a prince!" Even so, I'll wager she enlists the prince in rebuilding the Earth.)

Since, I'm exploiting family members, allow me one, further exploitation. Can you imagine how a blind, 26-year-old quadriplegic living her life in a wheelchair, can possibly be "in mission?" Let me introduce you to our granddaughter, Lindsey, who, since the age of two, because of an automobile accident, has been blind and confined to a wheelchair. I think she has more friends than I do, and after graduating from the Maryland School for the Blind, brought some of her friends together. They were all blind or severely disabled in one way or another. I can't tell you, *verbatim*, what Lindsey said, but I think it went something like this: "You know how other people are always helping us. Why can't we do something for other people?" That day, an organization came into being called "Friends." They've been meeting ever since, about once a month, for several years. They can't do anything very technical or skilled, but they can and do make tray favors for persons in nursing homes and care packages for persons in homeless shelters. "Friends," has a mission, and is an inspiration for a lot of people, including a grandfather who has learned that nobody has to be a victim all the time.

Well, those are examples from the semi-secular world. What about ecclesiastical change-agents renewing the institutional church from *within*? In my own denomination, I think of the caucus known as the Methodist Federation for Social Action, while in the other mainline, Protestant denominations, similar caucuses prophetically challenge institutions to take up the role of what Professor H. Richard Niebuhr called "the church as social pioneer."

I think of VIM, Volunteers in Mission, where teams of persons from local churches travel at their own expense to under-developed countries for the purpose of empowering other human beings to help themselves. You know how I learned about VIM? "The child is father of the man." Several years after I retired, the Reverend Christopher T. Holmes, who is now a District Superintendent here in the Baltimore-Washington Conference, but was then serving a church and was my pastor, said to me one day: "Dad, you ought to come with a group of us to Zimbabwe." He'd already been a number of times before, leading VIM teams. The conditions in Zimbabwe were and *are* unimaginable, and the experience was for me, transformational. VIM is the church being renewed from within.

This seminary is another ecclesiastical institution on the cutting edge, and a little later, Emeritus Dean Bruce Birch will be addressing its future. I want to mention just one aspect of its function pertaining to the gay/lesbian issue now roiling Roman Catholicism and almost all mainline, Protestant denominations. A seminary is an outpost of renewal when it not only teaches modern, biblical criticism – form criticism, hermeneutics, etc. – but also when it *prepares* students to teach such criticism to congregations. The church is in crisis over the gay/lesbian issue today primarily for one of two reasons: Either its clergy were never academically challenged by modern biblical scholarship, or its clergy were challenged, and have had a failure of nerve when it comes to helping congregations understand the scripture beyond literalistic interpretations: the Bible as "The *Word* of God" and not "the words of God."

This subject segues into another change agent now doing what the church should have been doing all along to address the biblical illiteracy of our own members. I'm referring to "The Jesus Seminar" which has as its primary mission the education of clergy and laity in how to read the Bible. Its biblical scholars are concerned to reconcile, on the one hand, the human need to know historically and scientifically, and, on the other hand, with the human need to create symbols and myths. And since many of the biblical myths we have inherited are at odds with aspects of our scientific knowledge, these scholars are going behind biblical texts to identify the primitive worldview from which ancient myths have come. They are showing how primitive myths are separate from Jesus' core message, and how that message can be communicated in our day through 21st Century myths and symbols compatible with modern science and history.

Presently, the Jesus Seminar is made up of 104 biblical scholars and 2,500 Associates, which include several of us in this Symposium. Through its popular "Jesus Seminars on the Road," the organization is reaching thousands of eager students. And, as one who has participated in several of those seminars, it is my sense that they are attended by as many or more laity as clergy. Best-selling authors John Dominic Crossan and Marcus Borg are as prominent in The Jesus Seminar as they are in the Society of Biblical Literature. Popular author-scholars such as Karen Armstrong and Bishop John Shelby Spong are Seminar contributors, and much of the Seminar's activities and outreach are occurring outside the institutional church – sometimes, in spite of it – while a majority of institutional Christians across our country remain biblically illiterate.

Last, but hardly least, the church is renewed, and thus the world is renewed, wherever clergy or laity set love in motion through speaking the WORD-EVENT. And that's not two words: "Word" and "Event" – it is one word hyphenated: "WORD-EVENT," with a two-fold, trip-hammer beat: WORD-EVENT, WORD-EVENT, WORD-EVENT! You know it when you've heard it!

It was this kind of preaching Karl Barth referred to as the "Protestant sacrament, the singular Word that has authority over everything else." It is an event described by Amos Wilder as a phenomenon where "God calls me, names me, addresses me." I can't ignore it or escape it. When you've been addressed, you know you've been addressed! To share in God's love, is to share in God's works of love in time and place, in the here and now. Martin Luther was right: "The church is a mouth-house..." And please note that's "mouth" not "mouse" (despite evidence to the contrary). Some years ago, P.T. Forsyth said in his Lyman Beecher Lectures at Yale, "With its preaching, Christianity stands or falls." "Faith cometh by hearing...." proclaimed the Apostle Paul. It did 2,000 years ago; it does today. That's the church renewed.

In closing, will you allow me one final indulgence: an old man's lament? I know something of homiletics, or at least I did in my own day. I taught it for a while at Perkins School of Theology in Dallas. I did post-graduate study in the subject at Union Theological Seminary in New York, where Paul Scherer used to say: "I don't care whether you preach from a manuscript, notes, outline, extemporaneously, or from memorization. I don't care whether you wear a suit, a robe, an alb, a chasuble or overalls. You can sit, stand, squat, kneel, and stand on your head, but I want to hear that Word which calls me into question, which confronts me and convicts me of my contemporary idolatry, which tells me who I am to God, and then catapults me into history to start building the world out of the love with which I have been loved."

That's the WORD-EVENT about which far too many laity and preachers don't have a clue. Not only are they at a loss as to how to talk about it and preach about it, they themselves have never been existentially confronted by its claim on their very own lives.

That's my lament. And thanks be to God there's an antidote, spoken by Brother Joe, as only Brother Joe could speak it:

> You have one mission: to love. Jesus wasn't sent to say God's love. He was sent to **be**, to **do** God's love. He was love divine, all love's excelling. Divine love always gets a stake through the heart; it always gets killed. That's your one vocation: being God's love in the world. Someone asks if you are a lawyer or a doctor or a minister. None of those are in the same ballpark of your vocation. Your vocation is to be divine love. That's your only assignment, and it always requires a decision – over and over again.

Including, I might add, the *decisions* that we make these next few days.

References cited:

Camus, Albert. Resistance, Rebellion, and Death; Alfred A. Knopf, New York, 1961.

Mathews, Joseph W. Bending History: Selected Talks. Resurgence Publishing, Lutz Fl., 33558, 2005.

Urban Mission:

Leadership Development with Global Vision

Bishop Felton E. May (retired), United Methodist Church

Bishop Mathews, Bishop Schol, friends, colleagues, co-workers, brothers and sisters all – you should know that I am honored and privileged to be with you in this gathering this evening, even as I stand here as a substitute for that great politician from 5th City, Congressman Davis, who is busy up on the Hill doing the work of government. Some of you I know very well, and others of you I have just met for the first time, but we are here because we are held together in this wonderful family of God by the legacy of Bishop James Kenneth Mathews and his brother Joseph Wesley Mathews, and their abiding spirit in Christ.

I wasn't sure what I would be saying to you, since I was originally scheduled for the presentation tomorrow morning, but I hope you will allow me a bit of latitude following that fine opening address by Bishop Schol. And I hope you will acknowledge that I have at least a little wisdom since I was on the Committee that affirmed the ministry of John Schol when years ago we appointed him to head the national work of the *Communities of Shalom*.

I want to begin this evening with Scripture, because it has been the very foundation of my own life and ministry, and though I have been accused by some with having a slight tinge of evangelical fervor, I need first to clarify that I also share considerable perspective on interfaith matters as well. What my biography doesn't say, but what you should know, is that I began as a young man serving for five years at a Reformed Jewish Temple on the South side of Chicago under the watchful eye of Rabbi Louis Leopold Mann, a brilliant professor at the University of Chicago who also led that congregation, where my task was simply to shepherd the evening programs in the office.

Rabbi Mann was **so** reformed that he held his services at 11:00 on Sunday mornings. It was so successful that people called the temple "Saint Sinai on the Lake." He used his own version of the liturgy, and he began a wonderful program for Christians and Jews working together, and on five Sundays every year he preached about the ministry and service of Jesus. It was a sixteen-hundred member congregation, with a 2,000 seat auditorium, and when he would preach his five-week sermon series on the mission and ministry of Jesus, there was not an empty seat in the synagogue.

One day when he was exiting his office, he said to me, "You will be doing the same thing soon," and I said "What?"

He said "yes -- I think God is calling you to be a minister, so why don't you go over to the Hyde Park community, and work at the St James Methodist Church where they want to start a church school program on Sunday afternoons, so you can be a teacher with young people." (It was already the first integrated church in the Rock River Annual Conference of the Methodist Church.) I said, "I don't know anything about that," and he said, "Doesn't your denomination have a bookstore?" I said "Yes, it's called Cokesbury." And he said, "Then go downtown to Cokesbury and find a book that tells you how to work with Junior High students."

I said "Yes Dr. Mann," and I did that – that was the beginning of my appropriating his global vision for mission and ministry

So I read about ministry and learned what it meant to be a child of God in service to the world. It has been a wonderful experience, and so I cannot help but offer a word of Scripture to put my remarks here tonight into context.

Reads: Luke 19:41 --

> "As he drew near and saw the city, Jesus wept. He wept over it, saying, "If you, even you, had only recognized on this day the

> things that make for Peace! But now they are hidden from your eyes. Indeed, the days will come upon you, when your enemies will... not leave one stone upon the other; because you did not recognize the time of your visitation from God."

These words went first to my eyes, then to my ears, and then to my heart. "He wept."

What words are these: "Would that you might do the things that make for peace." My mind instantly goes on to John 11, to the story of Mary and Martha and Lazarus, when they called on Jesus to raise their brother from the dead.

And when I think today about our own urban conditions, when I think of once healthy and vibrant cities, I weep -- because I am a city person. I have always lived in cities -- Detroit, Michigan; Chicago, Illinois; Wilmington, Delaware; Harrisburg, Pennsylvania; Washington D.C.; Little Rock, Arkansas; and now New York City.

I wept recently when my own family shared accounts about matters in Chicago, about young people with baseball bats, and guns, who walk the streets with murder in their eyes....

I weep for the city when I read reports about Detroit – the motor capital of the world, but now just a shell of a city -- where I spent most of my summers, working at the Bolar Publishing Company, owned and operated by my uncle and aunt.

Most recently I spent time with Bishop Devadhar and his staff. He is the Bishop of the Greater New Jersey Annual Conference.

Oh what a hell-hole Newark, New Jersey, really is... Drugs, prostitution, right in the brightness of daylight...on the main streets... Not just in the so-called "neighborhoods," but along the main thoroughfare of this once vibrant city – I wept as we drove in a van with the Bishop, his District Superintendents, and his Conference staff, through the devastation of that city, so I could see that now there are five churches where 20 years ago there were 23 United Methodist churches in the city.

Newark, New Jersey, is a mess -- a word that is an acronym for misery and evil living side by side. People <u>will live</u> – people will try <u>anything</u> to exist by any means necessary, even when it means selling one's own body, or taking from one another in such proportion that two of the largest, most well-built institutions in the community are funeral homes, where three or four funerals take place day by day.

And in its population, now largely African American and Hispanic, 80 percent of the people live in nontraditional families, some 8 or 9 to the room. The blocks are now occupied by McDonalds; where once full factories operated, they now have moved overseas. There are *no tenors singing in Newark*. (applause) But these *people will live* -- they will develop an alternative means of survival in the midst of alienation.

For the most part, urbanization is a euphemism for ghetto-ization. We have allowed the ghetto-izing of poor blacks and Latinos who now survive by working as keepers of small stores, fast-food establishments and gas stations.

The operative word is poverty... The U.S. does not have to choose between its own poor and addressing the needs of the world's poor -- it can do both at modest cost. There is much that we can learn from the social welfare states.... There are many success stories -- we know they have achieved a balance between public harmony and social institutions.

In his book <u>Common Wealth: Economics for a Crowded Planet</u>, Jeffery D. Sachs shows that we need a new economic paradigm -- global, inclusive, cooperative, environmentally aware and science-based -- because we are running up against the reality of a crowded planet. Jonathan Sachs is Director of the Earth Institute at Columbia University and special adviser to the Ambassador to U.N. Secretary-General Ban Ki-Moon on the Millennium Development Goals, so he is well-placed and well-informed about these matters.

He talks about the development of social insurance, not just for health issues, but <u>social</u> insurance for housing and food and medical care to help those in greatest need in a given geographical area.

He further states that "The world does not have to accept the continuing high rates of poverty as the price to pay for a vibrant market economy. Some social scientists have shown that market principles can be successfully combined with a highly efficient product distribution system so that people can prosper." The price of major corrections is small compared to our national income.

I hold those words before us as we begin tonight and soon celebrate a Star over Bethlehem, that will guide wise persons, who are willing to follow where the body of Christ can lead us.

We must think about our stake in this challenge, and step out into the light so that we can bring to an end this urban madness.

To help us along the way, I have garnered some thoughts from President Obama's message in accepting the Nobel peace prize. He spoke under the rubric of creating a world without poverty.

He states that some 90 percent of the world's income goes to 20 percent of the world's people and 60 percent of the world's people live on 6 percent of the world's resources. Half of the world's people live on less than $2/day, and one million live on less than $1/day.

The first time I heard these figures was in a speech by Bishop Mathews in which you, Sir, gave us the 80-20 formula: that 20 percent of the people control 80 percent of the world's resources, and **we** are a part of the 20 percent that enjoy the 80 percent abundance.

When I first heard that, chills ran down my spine.

Now -- I had heard those figures a few years earlier in Chicago from a man on the city's West side, talking about the struggles of people surviving in a strange place called 5th City.

I did not realize that Joe Mathews was your brother.

So at one of your teaching days, Bishop, you shared this information and showed us a pedagogy similar to what I had discovered in Chicago; and so at the break I came forward and said "I'm Felton May from Chicago, and I have learned a little bit of this same pedagogy from a man on the West side, living with a community in the ghetto.... Have you ever heard of him?" and you said, "I think so"... (laughter) Friends, he never went any further... I had then to discover Joe was your brother!

It was the genius of this teaching method that combines your imagination with the power of the Holy Spirit that compels us to act in a way in accordance with God's purposes.

Joe believed that putting resources in the hands of poor people is a better strategy than spending money on guns.... And so, because I am who I am, I am compelled to ask tonight, I ask -- is this what ICA is willing to do in our time?

Are you willing to take the government to task for perpetuating the conditions of poverty in cities across the world?

Your wisdom and methodology is on target, but my prayer here is that you will take what you know and the skills that you have and help create a government of the people, for the people, by the people in such a way that *God's Word will be enfleshed in our day*.

Poverty is the absence of motivation for using the resources for building a stable peace.

We have to find appropriate ways for people to live decent lives...

I want to share a bit more from this Nobel Peace Prize speech by the President, a wonderful oration about human capabilities... His words inspire us, but then we are confronted by the thoroughly inhuman constructs which prevent the blooming of these qualities rather than fulfilling the potential of God's people.

The President said, "We get what we want or what we expect when we accept the notion that poverty is part of human destiny." This is precisely why we continue to have poor people around us. I think it was Judas who first said that... It was when somebody was washing somebody's feet... Check that out. And the reason is -- somebody said in the Gospel of John that Judas was stealing some money for something else.

Could it be that the church with all its power and its programs, is banking on its "middle class-ism" while there are millions of people still living in urban cesspools around the country? Who is stealing the money? What do you call this obscene greed that has affected our lives like a cancer? Who will speak to it?

Will ICA talk about reforming the economic systems so that the poor will no longer need to be poor?

What we want and how we get there depends on our mindset... It is really difficult to change a mindset once it is formed. We create the world on the basis of our mindset

All it requires to get people out of poverty is to create an enabling environment that will permit the emergence of a new mindset.

There are organizations that we could coalesce with.... I'm talking about the United Methodist Church -- and any other religious entity in which we hold membership.

Have we ever thought about a coalition with the NAACP, or some other such organization that speaks for the poor, and is willing to share the pain and suffering of ethnic minorities?

Why not support a new approach to economic recovery with a mortgage protection agency, that will help the ethnic minorities -- they are the ones most hurt by this depression. It was black homeowners that were tripped up in mortgage arrangements that were unfairly and unknowingly thrust upon them – they are the ones in extreme difficulty.

What about cocaine sentencing? Drug sales are the No. 1 cash crop in distressed communities – but you know, *crack is not black*, and you know that those that are arrested for drug possession are disproportionately Black and Latino, and they get the stiffest sentences for possession of crack and crystal. The inequity is that our European brothers and sisters, our white brothers and sisters, are getting lighter sentences.... but this is nothing new – you know that already.

Some people say there are some Fortune 500 companies owned by well-heeled families operating in every black and Hispanic community in the country. I can't really say much about that, because I only know what I do from personal experience in some areas..... But I do see people suffering from the drug trade. How do you think they will live? They are forced to do what they're doing or else they will die. What about ICA, with its methodology, getting active in that arena?

Do you ever think about starting ICAs in prisons so that people there can talk with each other and learn about their God-given wisdom and talents so that when they exit prison the recidivism rate will not be so high? It pains my heart to see the waste of human lives.... But then, I'm just a crybaby.

I am a PACE Mississippi survivor, (applause) well... Bishop Mathews invited me to go down to Pace, Mississippi.... and he was a Bishop and I was a nobody, and so I said. "Yes, I'll go" – not knowing when I went that it had ICA behind it.

I didn't know anything about it until I was sitting there in a consult hall and saw all these people from Garrett Theological Seminary and the Ecumenical Institute coming through the door... it turned out to be one of the most amazing experiences I ever had -- probably my 14th conversion experience.

You know the history of ICA better than I do.... But I do know that the ICA process and programs can make a difference. And tonight we honor two men who might be considered the John and Charles Wesley of the 20th century.

I was simply molded to take a little bit of pedagogy and guided by the Mathews brothers... and subsequently was able to take it around the world, all because of the ministry of these two men and because of you.

And on those occasions, I have seen poverty in many places -- Sao Paulo, Rio, St Petersburg, Russia, Zurich, Switzerland, all across Africa and certainly in Zimbabwe. Even now, in the 21st century, millions of people the world over are still living in poverty. But, even now you have the vision and can help mobilize human resources so that not all of the poor in the cities of the world have to suffer.

The church should be doing this.... So much has been sanitized by General Conference... We say we want to be in ministry, but we do not think much about the pain and suffering going on in urban communities and we think we are going to be in ministry with them, but these programs make no contact with them, because our "do-good-ism" makes no connection.

I don't know what it would take to move beyond the programs to re-direct the genius of the United Methodist Church to get downright dirty... in a ministry focused on the world's poor..... I only know what I do from personal experience.

So I'll tell you something from my story: You know how we all re-write history – it's mostly to protect the innocent.... When I was first in Washington, I was assigned to develop a plan for addressing the drug problem in this city, the nation's capital city.

The Council of Bishops could send me anywhere, but they had to deal with my anger.... I rose one morning in the midst of that meeting of the Council and said "You had better find a place for me...."

I had seen a kid shot the night before, and just opposite on the television screen was the popular program about the Huxtables... you remember how sweet those stories were – each episode of the TV series with all African American characters... but I couldn't stand the sweetness.... And so I had the remote control in my hand, and I clicked over to CBS, to <u>48 Hours</u>, which was doing an *expose*' on the drug problems in our cities.

And so just out of the blue the Holy Spirit jabbed me in the back of the neck. The next day I stood and gave my report on Nicaragua and then said "You've got to do something with me... I'm sick and tired of churches and pastors who don't want to be the body of Christ, and are willing to ignore children dying on the streets of the nation's capital."

They didn't quite know what to make of it, never quite having dealt with a maverick bishop, but then Bishop Joseph Yeakel, who knows the <u>Discipline</u> better than anyone, found the right paragraph, where it says a Bishop can be set aside for special ministry.

My colleague sitting next to me whispered, "They're going to get rid of you." But then they voted yes.... they encircled me and laid their hands on me.... And Bishop Yeakel said, "You can use my building, maybe there's an apartment there...."

They voted to give me my salary and some travel. And so Phyllis and I packed up and moved to Washington. And I stayed there two years, uncharted, without any resources and without a plan.... I don't know where the plan came from – it just emerged.... but the staff responded, and we worked it out, and I got some resources....

All except one General Board.... You know, when you go to a General Board and ask for money... there ought to be some empathy when it is for the poor....

There was one General Board that was supposed to address poverty. But this one said, "Not on your life." I was told "You can speak at Chapel, but you can't speak at the board meeting...."

It was the General Board of Discipleship – of all the boards in the Church it is the one concerned with the needs of humankind telling them about a saving relationship with Jesus Christ.

Surely that would have been the one that would have responded.... But it got all tied up with politics... with in-fighting as bad as that between the Republicans and Democrats, dealing with health care needs for 40 million people in this country. But I am just a cry baby....

So here I am, assigned to Washington to address the drug problem, using a corrupted version of the ICA model to address the addictions of drugs and alcoholism.... And we managed to get people from some seventeen churches to come over to Shaw Church, and I went over to meet these 200 people, and was talking about how we should address drugs and crime in the city.

I was going on and on.... And a woman stood up and said "May I speak?"

And she said "I'm so-and-so, and our pastor told us he used to be an addict, that he is a recovering alcoholic for 30 years, and he goes to Alcoholics Anonymous, but then he came down and kneeled at the altar.... And I said "I am a recovering addict and a prostitute." And so I came forward and knelt there beside him.... So I want you to know, Bishop, that I have been clean for 7 or 8 years," and she kept on... "You know, Bishop, I hope you're a spiritual man, because if you're <u>not</u> a spiritual man you're not going to get to first base!"

And I thought to myself, "Who is she, thinking she can talk to a Bishop like that?" But she had made her point, and people were moved by it, moved to do some things.

The next morning I went over to St. Elizabeth's psychiatric hospital, the same place that John Hinkley was been kept, and met the Director, and some nurses and other staff. And he took me around the campus, and showed me where they help pregnant girls who are also addicts living on the streets.

Later, we were sitting around talking shop in his office. He said, very <u>politely</u> -- the way you're <u>supposed</u> to talk to a Bishop -- "Can I speak frankly to you?" He said, "We've got psychologists, psychiatrists, psychotherapists, social workers, doctors and nurses here.... They have their backs against the wall in dealing with these people or drugs, and there is a lot of that in the city, but if you're not a spiritual man, you don't have a chance...."

And I said to him, "You know, last night God spoke to me in the same way... and she said exactly the same thing...."

So I say to you tonight, "Have we got a foundation for addressing this? Have we left our anger? Have we left the one who will give us the resources and personnel, the passion and power far more than we ever dreamed or imagined?"

I have to find a way to make this point more forcefully because too often we find ourselves mired in legislative quagmires -- trying to maintain the institution just for the sake of maintaining what we've inherited. I mean: we end up saying we don't have money to do justice and mercy for those in the direst need....

We do know the things that make for peace.

The full import of the Mathews brothers' legacy will not be fully realized until there is the will and the commitment for ICA to collaborate with some others with vision who are willing to work within the church to change the policies that just build programs. We must find a way to adapt to the lifestyles of that particular ethnic community -- anywhere in the world, but especially here in our own country, especially in the cities....

It is the poor who need you. But somehow we lack the will to do it....

It appears to me that our global vision must be translated into a specific urban mission, but we must identify the factors that bring concrete improvements to people's lives. We will fail if we don't admit that do-good-ism only, no matter how well intended, will not win the day for Jesus Christ.

In the urban areas, Jesus still weeps over the plight of the city.

They thought Lazarus was dead, but the sisters sent word for Jesus to come, so Jesus got himself together, and Lazarus found new life....

So many think urban areas and ethnic groups are dead.... Or we call these people Neanderthal or write them off as "near death." But that's not the answer if we have a vision... because the one who said, "I am the resurrection and the life" must be our guide....

With the organizational brilliance of the ICA -- The Institute of Cultural Affairs -- could become an instrument of peace, with Christ's authority... Programs have had their day....

Let us act out the spirit of the Mathews brothers... if that Spirit will unite us, then we can do more than we ever dreamed or imagined....

The power of Christ must rest upon us and upon our institutions....

Then we can rise up with wings as eagles, run and not be weary, walk and not faint.

You say, "We can't do that, Bishop..." But -- ICA can do whatever it wants to do and if Brother Joe were here he'd say, "You're darned right we can do it."

If God be for us, who can be against us? Who can separate us from the love of God?

I'm just a crybaby... but with tears in my eyes I am convinced, following Paul in the 8th Chapter of Romans, that "neither death nor life, neither principalities and powers, nor things present, nor things to come, nor anything else in all creation, can separate us from the love of God through Christ Jesus our Lord."

In the name of my elder bother Jim, and his brother Joe, Let's do it... "In Christ's Authority".... That's the only ICA that really counts. Thank you.

Urban Mission in Wesley Seminary Education

Rev. Fred Smith, Ph.D., Professor, Wesley Theological Seminary

> *Seek the peace (Shalom) of the city... and pray to the Lord for it: for in its Shalom you will have Shalom* (Jeremiah 29:7)

Shalom is God's intention for creation. It is a state of wholeness which is an individual and collective experience of health, prosperity, security, justice, righteousness (right-relatedness as in oneness with nature and neighbor) and character. The components of the vision for theological education that will maximize those principles can be realized today in Urban Ministry. That is our goal as we create the Vision of Urban Ministry at Mount Vernon Square as an integral part of the curriculum at Wesley Theological Seminary in Washington DC.

Rethinking Seminary Education: Decentralized Campuses as Urban Laboratories

Centralized learning in monastic-like seminary campuses is facing a number of challenges. The first is that a significant number of students in seminary M.Div. programs today are second-career learners. These second-career students are part-time or full-time with mortgages, full-time jobs and family obligations that render relocating and residency requirements impossible to meet. Second, the economic crisis has challenged institutional endowments, and thus the ability to maintain expensive buildings and infrastructure on aging campuses (often located on prime property) is limited. Third, information and communication technology has made distance between educator and learner redundant and irrelevant. In the words of Maureen Bowman:

> The ways in which people form their identities and shape community is radically changing. Distributed learning is different from distance learning. Distributed learning includes distributed resources versus the predominant model of centralized campuses. *"Distributed learning is not just a new term to replace the other 'DL,' distance learning. Rather, it comes from the concept of distributed resources. Distributed learning is an instructional model that allows instructor, students, and content to be located in different, non-centralized locations so that instruction and learning occur independent of time and place. The distributed learning model can be used in combination with traditional classroom-based courses, with traditional distance learning courses, or it can be used to create wholly virtual classrooms."*

In a distributed learning model:

Students have greater amount of control over how, when, and where their learning occurs. They become responsible for their own learning instead of remaining passive receptacles of information and knowledge.

Faculty has the ability to create, organize and develop ministry opportunities that are praxis-oriented, with more freedom to experiment with effective new contexts for learning.

The seminary gains greater ability to allocate resources for learning opportunities. As Bowman says, "An abundance of research shows that alternatives to the traditional semester-length classroom-based lecture method produce more learning. Some of these alternatives are less expensive; many produce more learning for the same cost."

We are developing Urban Learning Laboratories all over the Northeast U.S. and other parts the country. Asbury United Methodist Church at 11th and K Street in downtown Washington DC, where the Urban Fellows program is based, is also where the office of the Urban Ministry Center for Community Transformation (CCT) is located. The next Urban Learning Laboratory will be in Baltimore City in partnership with the Baltimore-Washington Conference Hope for the City Urban Initiative. There are discussions taking place with other potential sites, in Syracuse, New York, in Camden/Wood-Lynne, New Jersey, in Richmond and Alexandra,

Virginia, in Memphis, Tennessee, in Pittsburgh, Pennsylvania, and even in Northern California. These sites will be located on a congregational-type campus and be hosted by a coalition of congregations or a jurisdictional body.

Dimensions in Seminary Urban Laboratories:

Any Urban Laboratory that becomes a center for seminary education should include in its planning and implementation most or all of these following dimensions.

- Community-to-Community mentoring
- Sharing resources and experience
- Technical assistance and training
- Ministry modeling
- Nurturing fellowship
- Support for CCT fellows
- A partnership with other congregations, Seminary and the communities.
- Host congregations to Urban Fellows
- Clearing house for promising practices in urban ministry.

Renewing Congregational Mission: Vision-driven Community-based Ministries:

The mission of the Church is to make disciples for transformation of the world. It is driven by a vision of the Kingdom of God. The Vision that drives the Urban Ministry Program at Mount Vernon Square known as The Urban Ministry Center for Community Transformation, is the *Beloved Community*.

The method of the theological education that seeks *shalom* is to draw on biblical and theological foundations to develop models which seek to redeem, restore and transform both congregations and their communities to create the Beloved Community. The Beloved Community is a metaphor for God's *shalom* expressed as a universal love ethic. This was first pictured by Josiah Royce as a community where love and justice rule in a community of distinct individuals who are loved for who they are in a plurality of their circumstances. Yet, they share a common memory and future. It is a community of interpretation where our stories, context and future hope have meaning and inspires hope and each individual is assured that they are loved.

Urban Fellows in Community Transformation Organizing and Developing Community through Small Group Ministries

Urban Fellows are a cohort of M.Div. and M.A. Students assembled in *intentional communities*.

- Their urban context becomes their primary textbook for their theological studies.
- They use Distance Learning technology.
- Theological education takes place in context.
- Students are recruited in and for specific communities.
- Their urban context becomes their primary text.
- Seminary education takes place on the main campus via intensive J-Terms (January) and during summer.
- Prophetic education becomes the primary pedagogy.
- Intensive learning experiences are based on Participatory Action Research (PAR) on the main seminary campus, with tutorial faculty guidance.

The Urban Ministry Fellows program engages in a *praxis* model of education. We believe that future urban ministers are best prepared by combining theory and "book learning" with hands-on practice within a supportive community to sustain theological reflection and faith formation. The Urban Ministry Fellows program at Wesley Seminary will fully embody this *praxis* model. We will be advancing our *praxis* model for urban ministry education by fully utilizing the downtown Washington D.C. community, based at our Mt. Vernon Place location, through deepening and expanding our partnerships with those area churches engaged in vibrant and effective urban ministry.

There are a number of churches in downtown D.C. that are engaged in faithful and fruitful urban ministry. There are many more who seek to be so engaged, but have limited capacity to do so effectively. Wesley Seminary's Urban Ministry Program seeks to partner with these churches both to provide *praxis*-oriented learning opportunities for its students and to benefit the churches by enhancing their capacity to undertake their urban ministry. We see this as a mutually beneficial and reciprocal partnership through which everyone learns, while engaging in urban ministry and through which we better equip our congregations to live into their call to urban ministry.

The Urban Ministry Fellows will participate in a pilot project of the Urban Ministry Program specially designed to support their development and training as urban ministers. The Fellows will participate in a year-long seminar that will introduce them to the downtown D.C. community and urban ministry *praxis* education model. They will learn about participatory action research methods — asset mapping, pastoral ethnography, and PIRHANA: Participatory-Inquiry-Into-Religious-Health-Assets-Networks-and-Agency, and apply these practices to the downtown D.C. community in order to introduce them to urban ministry and create networks for their future engagement in the community, such as Practice of Ministry and Mission (PMM) internship placements, mentoring relationships, and program partnerships. Their engagement in the downtown D.C. faith community will also contribute to Wesley's Urban Ministry Program's partnership development with the downtown congregations.

While there has been an Urban Ministries track at Wesley Seminary for decades, the new Urban Fellows Program is focused on the area around the Seminary's new presence at 908 Massachusetts Ave NW. Anchored by **Wesley's Urban Ministry Center for Community Transformation (CCT) at Mount Vernon Square**, and under the leadership of professors Fred Smith and Sam Marullo, five Master of Divinity students have served this year as the first cohort of Urban Fellows focused on urban ministry in downtown Washington D.C.

Faith-based organizations have a long history of working in D.C. to meet challenges like homelessness, hunger, violence, addiction, failed schools, inadequate health care systems and unemployment. In the midst of this ongoing economic recession when private donations and government support are in steep decline, faith-based organizations in D.C. are straining as they try to meet the increased need with less funding. In this climate there is great demand for **best practices, lessons learned, and opportunities for collaboration** in building strong communities and meeting the needs of the city's most vulnerable residents. One of the first aims of the Urban Fellows Program is to compile, organize and distribute information on the relevant resources in the community. The intention is that this will facilitate the work of D.C.'s faith-based communities, particularly in this time of need.

The Urban Ministry Center for Community Transformation

The Urban Ministry Center for Community Transformation *praxis* will include:

- ***Education***: Effective practice of ministry and leadership for transforming communities
- ***Collaboration***: Strategic partnerships for education, research and ministry
- ***Research***: Cutting edge knowledge of issues, practices, skills and models of congregational and community leadership

The goal is to build the Urban Research and Ministry Program to become one of the top five programs in the United States. The Urban Ministry Center for Community Transformation (CCT) theological focus is one of spiritual, moral and social transformation of communities according to biblical vision of the Reign of God. The CCT aims to ground students in the biblical vision of the Beloved Community so they will be equipped to transform the world in partnership with God. The Center's program will be church-based and grounded in biblical and theological reflection; social critical analysis; the social scientific research techniques and best practices in urban ministry.

The *praxis* and research of the Center will address such critical issues as: poverty, economic development and employment; affordable housing and homelessness; education and illiteracy; public health, health disparities and access to healthcare; families and at-risk children and youth; violence and substance abuse and addiction, and other issues associated with urban decay. The Urban Ministry Center for Community Transformation uses the best available social scientific knowledge and techniques, and provides students with a sound biblical and theological basis for conducting ministry in urban settings and to address issues often associated with urban problems.

One of the guiding principles of the CCT will be collaboration. The Urban Ministry Center for Community Transformation will seek to maintain viable, effective relationships between and among Center supporters, constituents, and other stakeholders. The Center foresees partnering with the Baltimore-Washington Conference of the United Methodist Church, and with local Washington and Baltimore congregations and ministerial alliances focused on the *shalom* of the of the Metropolitan area. The CCT has long-term aims for reshaping the urban church in order that it may better strengthen its community through a new capacity.

In Washington D.C. some of the most tragic urban realities proliferate and plague residents in this seat of national and global power and wealth: extreme rates of poverty and homelessness, with children the greatest victims; high rates of disease — some like tuberculosis have been cured in developing nations decades ago; unmitigated hunger, illiteracy, drugs, murder and violence. (Various reports cite the incidence rate of poverty and disease in Metropolitan Washington DC — a standard statistical region that includes Baltimore.)

Wesley's Urban Ministry Center for Community Transformation has the potential, through education and *praxis*, to become a visible example of the body of Christ *in praxis*, particularly in this urban community. The CCT aims to reshape the urban church to strengthen its surrounding community through a vision of the Beloved Community. Our mandate in urban ministry is to serve those who are most vulnerable, most at risk, and who are impoverished culturally, socially, economically, and most of all, spiritually.

Urban Ministry Symposium (Bi-Annual Conference):

The purpose of the Urban Symposium is to gather our collaborating partners, Practice of Ministry and Mission (PMM) sites, in order to highlight promising practices from around the country. The Symposium will serve multiple purposes, including as a recruiting opportunity for Wesley's Urban Ministry Program, for dissemination of research findings, as a forum for skill building opportunities, for networking and identifying opportunities for collaboration. The organization will include:

- Issue area tracks
- Inspiration, motivation and mobilization
- Training and technical assistance
- Networking
- Research dissemination
- Best practices
- Visioning

Leadership for Urban Ministry in the Joshua Generation

The theme of the opening symposium, "Leadership for Urban Ministry in the Joshua Generation," draws attention to the reality of the contemporary contexts of urban ministry. Just as Moses responded to God's call in a burning bush to free God's people from bondage in Egypt, so too have generations of leaders responded to cries of urgency and pain from the masses of God's people suffering the indignities of urban poverty, powerlessness, drugs, family dysfunction, violence, illiteracy, teen pregnancy, AIDS, homelessness, discrimination, and poor education. As Moses transferred leadership to Joshua, so a new generation of urban ministry leaders is emerging.

Just before Moses announced the choice of Joshua, he urged the people to "choose life." For our contemporary Joshua generation of urban ministry leaders, the choice is to cross the Jordan, roll up one's sleeves and continue the hard work of realizing Dr. Martin Luther King Jr.'s dream of the "Beloved Community."

Past generations have broken down barriers, opened doors, organized and advocated for change. However, poverty persists. Racial discrimination continues. Youth still drop out of school. Violence kills Black and Latino youth. Black males are disproportionately sentenced to prison. Families are failing. Homelessness is all around us. Serious challenges remain for this new generation. We are faced with the ongoing tasks of empowering the victims of injustice as well as challenging congregations and organizations to actively seek the liberation of persons, neighborhoods, cities – indeed, the whole nation -- from the bonds of social and economic injustice and inequality. This comes in the context of a wide-scale imperative to eliminate global poverty and injustice.

Conclusion:

The vision is to create Royce's Beloved Community, as envisioned by Rev. Dr. Martin Luther King, Jr., by fostering a presence of love, justice and right relationship for all God's people. The vision is lived out in the context of a new paradigm for seminary education involving a distributive *praxis* education model adaptable to communities of living and learning located in urban settings anywhere in the world.

The mission is to empower people in faith communities to improve the quality of the lives of the people in their larger community through education, research, and collaboration. This is accomplished through the involvement of seminary students in both theoretical and "hands on" learning processes as well as through direct work with clergy, laity, congregations and nonprofit organizations. Social justice issues which will focus research, education and collaborations include literacy and public education, faith and health, community and economic development, youth and family, environmental justice and elimination of local and global poverty.

The Urban Ministry Center for Community Transformation combines the use of the best available social scientific knowledge and techniques, promising practices in program operations and services delivery, and educating students with a sound biblical, prophetic, and theological base for conducting ministry in urban settings, to address the challenges often found there that separate us from God's Beloved Community.

The Urban Ministry Center for Community Transformation will operate as a resource center to support congregations; an educational center to train seminarians, pastors and lay leaders; a research center to create and disseminate knowledge; and a catalyst and resource for creating and sustaining effective collaborations. It will do this by mobilizing the distinctive resources and assets of Wesley Theological Seminary and the Center for Community Transformation stakeholders.

The resources we draw upon include the leadership, gifts, and expertise of the Wesley faculty and adjunct faculty; the talents, experience and gifts of the diverse students and alumni of Wesley; the many programmatic and personal connections among Wesley Seminary personnel and the local churches, including the readers of the *Wesley Connection*, the participants in the *Course Studies School* and those in the *Equipping Lay Ministry* program; the talents and experiences of our stakeholders in providing services and experiential learning sites for students; leveraging other strategic partnerships such as the Interfaith Health Program, American Association of Pastoral Care, Self-Help Center of Responsible Lending, and many other regional, national and international partners; the effective *shalom* ministries already operating in the Baltimore-Washington Conference and in our *Making Connections* network of seven United Methodist Church Annual Conferences.

The Urban Ministry Center for Community Transformation (CCT) will combine Wesley Theological Seminary's traditional urban ministry courses and its Practice of Ministry and Mission (PMM) model of contextual education, with applied research, and congregational and community collaboration to create a dynamic new form of "*praxis*-education." The new educational model will advance Wesley's mission "to equip Christians for leadership in the church and the world, to advance theological scholarship, and to provide a prophetic voice in the public square."

The CCT builds on, reconfigures and re-envisions Wesley's current urban theology program; strategically develops and expands the "*praxis* education" model which is already at the heart of Wesley's commitment to contextual education; deepens and expands Wesley's strategic commitment to be a congregationally-based seminary by linking Wesley students to urban congregations and to the communities which these congregations serve; and makes significant contributions to the discipline of practical theology. As a result we envision that Wesley will be among the nation's top five urban ministry programs by 2012.

Through the new Missional Church Center in downtown DC, the Urban Ministry Center for Community Transformation and Wesley's Public Theology Program will have unique opportunities to interconnect and support one another's objectives in the city of Washington and the national capital region, to literally and figuratively be a moral and prophetic voice in the public square for the city of Washington, the nation and beyond.

Acknowledgement: Dr. Fred Smith, Director, is the primary author of this article. He acknowledges the contributions from others on the staff of the Center for Community Transformation:

- Sam Marullo, Ph.D., Director of Research
- Hal Garman, Consultant
- Mary Beth Campbell, Consultant
- Adam Briddell, Program Assistant

References cited:

Bowman, Maureen. "What is Distributed learning?" in CSUMB Tech Notes, 27 April 1999, See http://techcollab.csumb.edu/techsheet2.1/distributed.html#endnotes.

Royce, Josiah. The Problem With Christianity. The Catholic University of America Press, Washington, DC. (originally published 1913, The Macmillan Company), 2001 edition. ISBN 0-8132-1072-0

Church Participation:

Numerical Decline in the Mainline Churches

Dean Snyder, Senior Pastor, Foundry United Methodist Church

It does not appear that the United Methodist church and other mainline denominations are doing well numerically.

Why does there seem to be such numerical decline and so little growth? I do not buy the argument that numerical growth is proof of correct theology and decline is proof of wrong theology. If so, we should all become Mormons or internet pornographers. Growth and decline are not determined by whether we are liberal or conservative.

Years ago, when I was a Conference director of congregational development, I invited the pastors of the forty churches that had reported the greatest attendance growth over the past decade to meet with the bishop and other Conference leaders to tell us why they were growing. The churches were invited to the discussion because their attendance had increased the most -- these included every theological variant of the Conference.

When I directed congregational development, I was fairly single-minded. I didn't care if a new-church-start pastor was conservative or liberal. My only questions were whether he or she had the capacity to build a congregation and whether he or she was loyal to United Methodism. It seemed to me that no single theological perspective had a greater capacity than others to start churches. This is also what Steve Compton seems to suggest in his book Rekindling the Mainline: New Life through New Churches.

I believe that the numerical decline the United Methodist Church is facing has to do with non-theological issues, and it seems to me these are the most significant ones:

1. *Clergy are not expected or trained to grow churches*. For the most part, bishops and district superintendents don't communicate to pastors an expectation that their churches should be reaching new people and growing. Instead, they may well communicate that what they want is happy, non-complaining congregations.

Cultural and missional shifts that help stagnated congregations grow often include discomfort. Some clergy do really dumb things down in the name of growth and wound or destroy congregations. Many more clergy accommodate congregations, allowing them to gradually decline. Bishops and district superintendents tend to get more upset about the former than the latter. I know of no pastor who has ever gotten a phone call from his or her superintendent saying, "You've been at your church two years now, and I haven't heard any complaints about your ministry. Why not?"

For the most part, seminaries -- which tend to belong more to academia than to the church -- don't teach students how to grow churches. Most faculties know much more about how to maneuver in the academic world in order to get degrees than they know about how to grow churches. Unlike medical schools and law schools, our seminaries have very few successful practitioners on their faculties. Furthermore, in order to support themselves, many seminary students take appointments to small congregations where they learn to be chaplains rather than leaders.

You can spend an entire career in the United Methodist ministry getting appointments one after another without ever being told it is your job to help congregations grow, or returning for continuous training about how to do so.

2. *High maintenance laity hold many of our congregations in bondage*. Often these are persons, families, or cliques for whom the

congregation is an important place to meet their needs for inclusion, recognition, and power. They do so at the expense of welcoming, including, or empowering others. Meetings in many congregations are hijacked by individuals with extreme needs for attention and control. Others may have poor social skills so as to turn meetings or classes into unproductive or unfocused sessions.

Councils and boards can meet month after month and accomplish little because of one or two dysfunctional members. No one is able -- often no one even tries -- to set limits on the dominance of dysfunctional individuals in small groups over congregations. No one insists they get help. Congregations become no fun. These members help create congregations that thwart spiritual growth rather than enhance it.

3. *Our real estate often limits growth.* Church buildings that hold only small numbers of people; have grossly inadequate space for Christian education; have little or no parking; look dirty, cluttered, and ugly inside -- and are at the wrong locations -- hinder growth. Other buildings that are beautiful but not functional hinder growth. Emotional attachment to buildings that prevent congregations from relocating in order to reach out to and serve new people hinders growth. Buildings that are allowed to deteriorate while a small group holds on as the neighborhood changes without reaching out to the nearby new people hinders growth.

Howard Snyder says in a *Christianity Today* article: “Interestingly, church history shows an inverse ratio between dynamic church multiplication and preoccupation with buildings.” Snyder writes: “Emphasis on buildings is generally linked with relatively slow growth or even decline. Rapidly growing movements generally put little stress on buildings, tending toward pragmatism and flexibility, meeting wherever they can.”

4. *We aren't starting nearly enough new congregations,* new campuses for the expansion of existing churches, and multiple services. New churches, new campuses, and new worship services reach new people.

I attended a training recently where I was the only clergyperson participating. One of the other participants who was active in the leadership of a new, very conservative mega-church asked me a lot of questions about my congregation. At the end of the training she told me she would love to belong to a church like mine where she could say what she really thinks. Often she has to stifle her real thoughts and feelings to “fit in” at her church, she told me. I asked her why she didn't join a United Methodist church in her community. “Oh, there wasn't room for me in those churches,” she said. “I wanted to find someplace where I could make a real contribution.”

Lyle Schaller says in The Ice Cube is Melting (p. 31) that to remain on a plateau in size a denomination should organize as many new congregations each year equal to one percent of the number of existing congregations. The United Methodist Church has 350,000 congregations, so to stay the same size we should be starting 350 churches a year. For us to grow would require even more. The actual number of new United Methodist church starts since 1965 has averaged out to less than 75 per year.

This is how Bishop Will Willimon summarizes it: “Growing denominations have higher rates of new-church development and an increasing average congregation size. Growing denominations plant churches in areas that are 'geographically favorable' -- that is, in areas of high population growth, high in-migration rates, and/or unchurched people groups.... We United Methodists, in my opinion, confirm these hypotheses in that we have a huge number of very small congregations, a decreasing number of large congregations. We tend to have a high proportion of churches that were in areas of population growth a century ago, but are in areas of population decline today.”

5. *We have low standards of quality*. Worship, preaching, music, Christian education, printed materials, and responsiveness are too often second-rate in our churches, and we don't seem to notice or care. I once knew a church secretary who had the highest quality office equipment available, but still produced Sunday bulletins that looked like they had been mimeographed. This was the way bulletins looked when she was growing up, and this is the way she thought bulletins ought to still look today. She worked hard to make her excellent equipment turn out bulletins that looked like the ones she read in church in the 1950s.

While I think growth is equally possible in liberal, middle-of-the-road, and conservative congregations, I do not think ongoing conflicts like our current debate about sexual orientation help us, especially when we are so divided about the issue that we do not do a good job of interpreting it to the unchurched. Personally, I would rather be part of a denomination that wrestles with difficult questions, and I think some others out there in the unchurched part of the world would prefer this too.

We should explain to the world around us that our disagreements are healthy. We should proudly say that it is a good thing that United Methodists do not hide our heads in the sand, that we do not duck the hard issues, and that we are not automatically closed to considering change. Without this kind of interpretation, the unchurched who read about church trials and such ask either, "How can Methodists be so backwards?" or else "How can Methodists be so freewheeling?" We do not (excuse the word) *spin* this story well. Lately, forces within United Methodism have become so intent on stopping even the talk about sexual orientation that church agencies and communication arms are now too intimidated to speak about the good aspects of being part of a denomination where we can disagree.

Yet, even our disagreements are relatively small matters compared to the other reasons I have listed. If our clergy aren't motivated and encouraged to grow their churches, if two or three laypersons are allowed to dominate church life destructively, if we are stuck in buildings that cannot accommodate growth, if we are not starting new congregations, and if the quality of our worship, music, and programs is second rate, why should we expect to grow?

References cited:

Compton, Steve. Rekindling the Mainline: New Life through New Churches. The Alban Institute: www.alban.org.

Howard A. Snyder (4/28/2005) "God's Housing Crisis," Christianity Today, July 29, 2010, http://www.christianitytoday.com/ct/2005/may/24.54.html

Schaller, Lyle E. The Ice Cube is Melting. Abingdon Press, Nashville. 2004.

Church Participation: Numerical Decline

Hauerwas, Stanley & William A. Willimon. Resident Aliens. Abingdon Press, Nashville, 1989.

Eternal Values in a World of Change

Bishop Susan M. Morrison (retired), The United Methodist Church

Grace and peace to you --the remnant -- snowbound but hopefully spirit-led. I feel like I have been in the middle of an Ecumenical Institute (E.I.) alumni meeting. Though I have a relationship with the E.I. and the Institute for Cultural Affairs (ICA), I am less connected than most of you. I am impressed by your spirit, and the warmth and humor I experience, expressed especially about that old curmudgeon and guru, Joe Mathews. It has been fun to experience.

I especially remember Bishop Felton May speaking of Jim and Joe Mathews as the modern John and Charles Wesley. Personally, I have always called Jim and Eunice Mathews the last of Methodist royalty. This is because of the scope of their witness and mission: the reaching across cultural and religious boundaries to meet and dialogue with constructive results some of the great historical figures of our time. Why, I even remember Bishop Jim telling of meeting by happenstance Mohammed Ali on a plane. I am proud to say that Jim and Eunice have been my parents in the faith.

I. Re-thinking Church

It seems so appropriate for us to gather here and honor the Mathews brothers. For you who are United Methodists, you may be aware of the latest institutional campaign called "re-think church." Besides a variety of promos like training events and items with the words "re-think" to be purchased (mugs, shirts, fleeces, etc), you may have seen ads on TV being run with this theme.

The campaign's goal is to show people -- those seeking spiritual meaning -- that within the church's mission of world transformation they may find hope. It attempts to use "out of the box" -- out of the usual -- institutional models, ways to tell the church's story, pointing out the church's action in the world of easing human suffering, feeding the spiritually and physically hungry, and spreading hope. It is an attempt to be relevant today with a message especially to folk outside the church or those dissatisfied with the current one.

I want to say, "Well, HELLO!!" This is what the Mathews brothers have been doing all their lives -- continually re-thinking church. I remember a scene at one of our College of Bishops meetings when, as we were probably droning on, the oldest in the group spoke up. It was Jim. And one of my colleagues shook his head and said to me, "Another fresh idea. It never ceases to amaze me!"

It is an honor to be participating in this event, for both Joe and Jim have had a significant impact on my life and faith journey. I was, to use a now somewhat questionable label, a "child of the sixties." If there was a protest movement against some injustice, I was there. Through a wonderful campus ministry program I began to connect a growing faith to social involvement and to become aware that evangelism could mean more than knowing and telling stories of Jesus.

Bishop Jim put it well in a speech he gave at Boston University School of Theology (where a Chair of Evangelism has since been named for him and for Eunice): "Nowadays the typical evangelist... is so anxious to speak that he/she too quickly turns to the WORD of the Gospel. In the New Testament all four of the Evangelists do the opposite. They first speak of the DEEDS of Jesus, addressed to real human needs, but raise also the question, Why? The WORD of God then becomes relevant."

II. The Legacy

Through my campus ministry experience and the DEEDS model of Jesus, for me there developed a strong sense of call to mission. In talking to my campus minister one day, I learned that there was a person coming that week from the UM Board of Missions who was looking for young people for teams to serve in urban Brazil and in rural Bolivia. I applied. An interesting footnote to that application process is that I was asked if I smoked or drank -- but nothing concerning if I were baptized or a church member. I was neither. When they belatedly discovered that, it was rectified and I was accepted for the Brazil team. But thereafter, they changed the form!

At our missionary orientation, one of the key leaders was Joe Matthews. His presentations had a deep influence on the life and mission of our team in Brazil. He was a strong and articulate proponent of needing community and of having a common life together with the discipline of prayer, study, and action. There were six Americans on our team and we realized the needs of Brazilians. Throughout our three and one-half years there, between 10 and 12 members, American and Brazilian, worked in a slum community near Rio. I am convinced that the discipline of the daily order made ALL the difference in gathering together such a diverse group of personalities and enabling us to be as effective in our mission as we were. Our team ministry became a model for the Brazilian church and has been used in various places around Brazil in the years since then. Brazilian members of our team have also provided significant leadership in the church there through the years, including serving as an elected Bishop and a seminary president.

Also, like others who have spoken before me, the religious studies, RS-1, for instance, was crucial for my faith development. I, too, used the charting as a way of studying papers all through seminary. One story comes to mind: After our overseas orientation, held in Stony Point, New York, our team spent time at the Ecumenical Institute in Chicago. I remember the picnic tables, the oranges, and the cold cereal for breakfast. I remember sleeping in bunk beds, and I remember a knock on my door around 6:00 one morning followed by the words, "Christ is Risen!" And as the early morning "crier" moved on to the next room, knocking on the door and repeating the phrase, "Christ is Risen," I heard a voice from within the room, answering, "The Hell He has!" Both Joe and Jim assumed God was wide awake if they were! Jim was notorious in the conferences he led for his very early morning phone calls.

I remember Joe as being a somewhat gruff figure, yet in a conversation with a woman (at Stony Point) who was commenting about her disapproval of Christians dancing, Joe's response was, "Oh, Ma'am, all good Christians ought to know how to dance!" (It's interesting, isn't it, what stays with you.)

I'm grateful for Joe's life and witness. There have been so many ecumenical settings I have been in through the years where the denominational leaders have been influenced in their ministries by the work of the Ecumenical Institute.

III. Eternal Values

Bishop Jim Mathews wrote that a Christian is called to a life of holiness -- a holiness not of escape but of engagement. That certainly was how he modeled his ministry in the Episcopacy to those who served with him.

I was a newly appointed, first-time pastor in the Baltimore-Washington Conference when I received an Episcopal letter inviting all pastors to "Study Days" in the District. In that era, "invitations" were command performances. And for three years, twice annually, pastors met with Bishop Mathews for what he called "an unhurried day of serious study." We covered doctrine, social principles, peace and self-development of peoples. In several of the study days we reflected on the Holy Life and its meaning for our time.

This led to a study of some depth, District by District, of devotional classics, some ancient, some modern. Bishop Matthews made it clear that this was neither an escape from nor a turning in upon oneself. It was an engagement on behalf of the world and was to address in intercession and active service the crying needs of real people. From these studies, a committee of clergy, including myself, developed a daily office, called *Deeper Furrows*, that was put in book form and distributed throughout the Conference for use by all clergy.

As I read *Eternal Values in a World of Change*, the years-ago experience with Bishop Matthews came clearly to mind. As has already been mentioned, one of his great gifts in the Episcopacy was his engagement in the teaching role of the office. This book is a teaching tool. Share it. Talk about the ideas in the book. It is helpful to know what a person thinks, helpful to know what motivates them to ACT.

IV. Current Crises

Bishop Jim begins *Eternal Values* by lifting up issues of concern facing the world. What immediately struck me was how relevant today are the issues he raised. I was asked to discuss how this book could serve as a teaching model. He uses stories, so I will share some of them also.

First, an aside: while the manuscript I received had no date, the picture of the author accompanying the book is of a young, dashing-looking gentleman and the bio information indicated he was serving as associate General Secretary of the Board of Missions of the Methodist Church. (That's now called the General Board of Global Ministries.) So I researched it: the book was published in 1960, fully 50 years ago.

Now, continuing. Jim talks about the shrinking world. In the situation, we can either feel compressed and confined or we can reach out and embrace an ever-larger world. There is a wonderful line in a story he tells in *Eternal Values* (see page 2) about one of his daughters preparing a school report after visiting South America with her father. In it she said, "I found people friendly to me everywhere; they were only waiting to meet me so we could be friends." It is a quote, and a learning, that could serve us all, as we become more and more global citizens, as we find ourselves in situations of engagement with other cultures and other religions. *They've been waiting to meet us so we could be friends.*

And then he touches on the profound separation among humankind, when our age demands unity. Just to read the headlines of papers, we know the reality of separation still exists today in nationalism, religious conflict, or racial tensions. All of these he addresses. He tells the story of a friend who visited Macao, the tiny Portuguese-established colony off the south coast of mainline China. While there he was able to get a glimpse of the Chinese mainland. And quite a glimpse it was! As he lifted his binoculars to look toward China, he looked directly into the gaze of a Chinese officer training his binoculars right on him! The tools of looking suspiciously at the "other" are different today, with satellites, sophisticated listening devices, and computer break-ins. But we know distrust still exists, often with tragic results.

I was reminded of all that as I listened to President Obama's speech accepting the Nobel Peace prize (as reported in USA Today). He said,

> "...Wars between nations have increasingly given way to wars within nations. The resurgence of ethnic or sectarian conflicts, the growth of secessionist movements, insurgencies and failed states have increasingly trapped civilians in unending chaos. In today's wars, many more civilians are killed than soldiers; the seeds of future conflict are sown, economies wrecked, civil societies torn asunder, refugees amassed, and children scarred."

President Obama says that the hard truth is we will not eradicate violent conflict in our lifetime and then he quotes Dr. Martin Luther King, Jr. when once he received the Nobel Peace Prize *(USA Today)*, saying,

> "Violence never brings permanent peace. It solves no social problem. It merely creates new and more complicated ones."

Reflecting on the reality of the human drama, Bishop Mathews lifts up the dilemma that while humans might be conquering space, they have not conquered themselves. The basic problems of selfishness and tensions in human relationships remain. He writes (page 7),

> "We hear nowadays not only of problems of outer space, but also of inner space, of emptiness in the midst of plenty, of oppressive guilt without any bill of particulars, of anxiety without apparent cause, of meaninglessness, of estrangement, of one's sense of alienation without logical foundation."

Yet he doesn't end the conversation here. He goes on to say that we need not be cynical, defeatist, or pessimistic, for while we lift up these challenging characteristics of our time we need to remember that this time is really God's time. And it is a time for us to decide. Yes, we are undergoing a profound shaking of foundations.

But that is not the last word, the last reality. He says that there is something that is unchanging that can anchor us in the midst of uncertainty and newness, of distrust and human dilemmas. This "something " is the eternal values that are constant for people of faith, values that are not simply about abstract standards but are solid principles that arise out of concrete situations of life and in our relationships with others. We have to actively participate to grasp their importance.

One of my most vivid memories of Bishop Matthews at Council of Bishops meetings is of his way of going to the mike as we debated all the problems and needs of the institutional church and his reminding us that those problems are not the last word. He would have something upbeat to say. He would remind us that God is present, that there is much for which to be grateful and that there is much that gives us hope <u>while there is still much to do</u>!

V. The Six Values In Today's Context

The book lifts up six eternal values for our consideration.

<u>First, there is the Unshakable Kingdom</u> (Realm). (I'll give Jim a pass on inclusive language.) This realm is the understanding of a ruling God who is not a way-off God but one who is "personal, compelling, and all embracing." Our response to this very present God is to be responsibly and actively in the world. He says that this Realm as set forth in the Gospel message does not advocate status quo, is devoted to change, carries messages of new birth and of leaven that transforms the whole.

Bishop Jim says the idea of the Realm was not new when Jesus came but that it was a reign of the future. Jesus claimed it was <u>near</u>, immediately at hand, actual, absolute, personal, compelling and all-embracing. And the Realm is within. The emphasis is on the accessibility of the Realm to each one of us. It is accessible to all. At the same time, this "realm" puts heavy demands on us. It is not characterized by sweetness and light, but is characterized by labor and fortitude. We may live in a world of change but we owe our allegiance to a God and to a realm that cannot be shaken.

Bishop Jim used an illustration (page 11) that is dated, but still useful. He was at a meeting where a prominent Nigerian Christian leader pointed at the Americans at the conference and said, "What are you going to do about Little Rock?!" Well, Bishop Mathews and Bishop Golden <u>had/did</u> try to do something. By attempting to worship at Callaway UMC in

Jackson, Mississippi, they may have been physically turned away, but their witness and the message it gave is remembered today.

What are we doing about the "Little Rocks" of today? What are we doing about the crisis points that need our witness? Bill Holmes challenged us well yesterday. I can say I am proud of the Council of Bishops' two statements issued last month, one regarding the environment called *In Defense of Creation,* and one on the war in Afghanistan.

The second value lifted up is that of an Unchanging Lord who is our eternal contemporary. Jesus is at home in every age. Mathews' emphasis is that as we know this Jesus, we know who we are. It is in relationship with God and with others that our own sense of being becomes clear. As the New Testament makes clear, Jesus is not only a unifying character but a unifying theme.

Eternal Values has a wonderful quote (page 16-17) from *Dr. Zhivago* regarding early Rome and the transformation Jesus brings in any age:

> "Rome was a flea market of borrowed gods and conquered peoples; a bargain basement on two floors, earth and heaven; a mass of filth filled with people with eyes sunk in fat, sodomy, double chins; illiterate emperors, and fish fed on the flesh of learned slaves. And then, into this tasteless heap of gold and marble, He came, light and clothed in an aura, emphatically human, deliberately provincial, and Galilean. And at that moment gods and nations ceased to be and [humans] came into being: Man the carpenter, Man the plowman, Man the shepherd with his flock of sheep at sunset, Man who does not sound in the least proud, Man thankfully celebrated in all the cradle songs of mothers and in all the picture galleries the world over."

There is power in that imagery. It connects with us today. Think about the unchanging Lord and transforming Lord who is the same yesterday and today and forever.

Then there is the story Mathews tells (page 24) about the woman living in Brazil (one that has special significance for me perhaps because of my Brazil connection.) Dominating the city of Rio de Janeiro, on top of a high mountain, is a statue of Christ the Redeemer standing with outstretched hands. Very often, as close as it is to the sea, the figure is obscured by fog and clouds. There was living in Rio a Methodist woman very ill with cancer. She was treated for a while in hospital and finally told that her disease was incurable. She had been staying in the home of a friend in Rio while in treatment. Her friend observed to her that ever since she had been there the clouds had obscured the figure of Christ, and went on to say, "Won't you stay a little longer, until you can finally see him?" The ill woman's response was, "I know Jesus Christ, who dwells in my heart, and no cloud can obscure him."

The third value is that of an Imperishable Message. In this section Jim draws on his experience as a missionary and reflects on how the message gets translated. He writes of the recognition of differences in other cultures and in religious traditions and how that recognition helps us understand them, tempering our attitudes towards them, leading us to go to others in deep penitence. He says that we need go in deep modesty, not to force or compel. We go with humility because we go as BEARERS, not POSSESSORS of a gift. We go because Jesus commanded us to go.

And what is the Gospel message? It is not simply a biography of Jesus, nor a memoir written by apostles, nor a set of ideas about God, nor just a philosophy or way of life. It is not just teachings, not just mysticism or a metaphysical principle. The Gospel IS what God DOES as God acts redemptively for all people. The Gospel is God meeting us in Christ, offering Godself to us, demanding and enabling our response and commitment. It is what Martin Luther called the "Gospel in miniature" in John 3:16, "for God so loved the world...."

Mathews, as he often does, uses story (page 28-29) to show how the imperishable message gets connected to folk, how it may change with the times, especially addressing the missionary movement. He speaks of visiting Oxford University. When its buildings were being built, it was thought they would last a long time. Not so. Along walls you can see holes; you can see crumbling areas. So the walls are slowly being rebuilt. It takes time, but while the rebuilding is going on, so is the work of the University. Jim says this a parable for the missionary movement today.

The founders of the modern mission movement thought their methods would last forever. Not so. While we attempt to change the methodology, the missionary task continues. The scaffolding, the framework, the techniques all change, but the message is imperishable.

I thought of that illustration as I read a recent newspaper (USA Today, 12.10.2009). An article said that a survey by the Pew Forum on Religion and Public Life, showed that elements of Eastern Faiths and New Age thinking have been widely adopted by 65 percent of U.S. adults, including many who call themselves Protestants and Catholics. "Mixing and matching practices and beliefs is as much the norm as it is the exception," Pew's Alan Cooperman said.

The last three values come from the well-known message set forth in First Corinthians by Paul: faith, hope and love. Our **faith** is trust in God and our response to what God does for us. It is confidence that we are God's children and part of God's action in the world.

Again, Mathews uses story (page 41-42) to emphasize one's trust in faith. He tells of the great Scottish preacher, Alexander Whyte, who determined never to take into church any member who could not recite the creeds and evidence knowledge of the doctrines of the church. Then an elderly woman came wanting to join the church. He asked her one doctrinal question after another; she didn't know the answers. Whyte wanted to discourage her, but then she said about Jesus Christ, "I do not know the answers to these questions, but I would die for the love of him!" Faith was sufficient.

Jim Todhunter, retired United Church of Christ pastor, (quoted in USA Today, 12.10.2009) says:

> "In the Western religions – Judaism, Christianity, and Islam – the focus is: What do you believe? There is always a tremendous focus on doctrine and teachings. In the East, Buddhism and Hinduism in particular, the leading question is: Do you know God? It is much more experience based."

Faith is the blind one seeing, the deaf one hearing, the dead one coming alive. Like the healing stories of Jesus, faith is recognizing the great work Jesus Christ has done in our lives.

Jim's whole missionary ministry is a clear example of the living out of faith and living out of trust in God.

"Hope Endures" is another value. It gives us vision and encourages us to go forward with genuine anticipation. Hope is especially meaningful in times of great change. It can even be said that change is an expression of hope.

Most all of us live with some hope. Jim tells the story of sitting next to a woman who barely escaped Communist China with her life. She said she didn't feel safe anywhere. She was afraid of reprisals on her parents still living on the mainland. When Jim asked "Where is your hope?" her reply was, "You forget I am a refugee ... we have no hope." Grim words! Think of all the refugees today, especially those in camps. In Obama's speech, he says, "The absence of hope can rot a society within."

Christian hope is a hope in God. The Psalmist says, "Hope in God, for I shall yet praise God, who is the health of my countenance, and my God." (Ps. 43:5, KJV) Christian hope rests in resurrection, in the Living Lord. Mathews quotes John Calvin, saying "the church's history is a history of continuous resurrection."

I have to tell you, that quotation amused me! As a person involved for most of her ministry in the institutional church life, I was reminded of the plethora of ways we have tried to "resurrect ourselves." From quadrennial emphases, missional themes, and liturgical experiments to numerical goals and priority askings; from primary tasks and ministry plans to structural changes and visionary task forces; from spiritual renewal and developmental guidelines to Episcopal declarations, pathways and four foci, we are constantly "making ourselves anew." I don't think that is what Calvin meant by resurrection "happening."

I want to say here that Bishop Mathews' ministry in the episcopacy brought hope to many a woman who felt called to the ordained ministry. I believe there is no one in the United Methodist Church, or in any denomination, for that matter, who has had such an impact on the role of women. I was one of the first ordained. The bishop (not Mathews) who ordained me deacon was on record as discouraging women. He preached at my special ordination (there was just me, a deacon and Felton May, an elder) and he spoke of the future of the church as men in ministry, clearly not using "men" as a generic term. In contrast, Bishop Mathews opened the church pulpits to women, and helped the seminaries in his area cultivate women pastors. The Baltimore–Washington Conference Clergywomen was the largest contingent from any conference when the denominational clergywomen met in New Mexico in 1980. Their music is known across the church.

The Christian is a person of faith, of hope and of LOVE – the sixth eternal value. The New Testament makes it quite clear that we are loved by God. This is our identity. And therefore, we are those who must love others. This is our role in life. And the gospel teaches us that God loves and accepts us AS WE ARE.

Joe Mathews (quoted in *Eternal Values*, p. 57) writes,

> "Sometimes we say we are accepted by God because we repent. This is sheer nonsense. Quite the contrary is true. It should be said that we repent because we are accepted by God; for there would be no point in turning to [God] unless the Word had come to us that God loves us as we are. At other times we say to ourselves God does not love us for what we are, but for what we can become. This, too, is nonsense. For if [God] loves the one we can be, God loves someone who does not exist; God does not love US. The whole gospel shouts that [God] loves us as we are. So the Christian invitation is "Come as you are." When we do, a miracle takes place. When we are willing to be who we are and come to God as we are, we are made into someone different."

God loves us and accepts us as we are. God also expects us to love and accept others as they are. This completely revolutionizes all human relationships. Our attitude toward other people does not depend on who they are but upon who we are. In the parable of the man who fell among robbers, that person is not named. Someone has observed that he is perfectly anonymous so that he is perfectly universal. This means, then, our neighbors are every person.

I think of all the ecumenical and interfaith involvements of which Bishop Mathews has been a part, of the leadership he has given, of his commitment to all of us being connected, to living the reality that ALL are our neighbors.

Mathews tells the story of Mahatma Gandhi traveling to London for a Round-Table Conference. He could have stayed in a large hotel or even have been a guest of the state. Instead, he accepted the invitation of Muriel Lester, who had a settlement house (called Kingdom House) in the slums of the East End of London. It was already crowded, but they made room for him. As Gandhi reported, "Love makes room where there isn't any!" (*Eternal Values*, p. 60).

Love is inclusive. It is therefore, missionary. For faith compels us, and hope draws us, and love gives us away.

Mathews closes (p. 61) by saying,

> "For the Christian there is no place too far. There is no need too deep. There is no barrier too high. There is no pride too great. The mission will carry one to the end of the earth and across every frontier of society. But one doesn't go alone. For when Jesus says, 'Follow me', he simply means, walk the same road that I walk."

VI. Endless Engagement

One last story. As Bishop I was assigned to the Philadelphia Area. This included two conferences, Eastern Pennsylvania and Puerto Rico. There was a growing movement to change the status of Puerto Rico, to have it become more independent, to have its own Bishop. I worked with the Puerto Rico Conference to develop its own constitution.

When the meeting was held in the Northeast Jurisdiction to vote on Puerto Rico's new role as a new area, the votes were there. That was no mystery. The conversation was instead, who will serve as Bishop of the new area until at the regular time a new Bishop would be elected? Folks needed something on which to speculate.

After the vote, when the meeting was adjourned, we bishops moved up onto the stage to be closer together. I sat there with tears filling my eyes, grieving the change, grieving the loss of Puerto Rico. Meanwhile, up there on the stage, Jim Mathews was "bopping around," grinning and shaking hands with everyone in sight. No one needed to ask who would serve the new area. It was obvious.

Remember that early Mathews quote? "A Christian is called to a life of holiness, a holiness not of escape but engagement."

All quotes from Bishop Mathews' book are from Mathews, James K. *Eternal Values in a World of Change*, 2nd ed. 2009. Resurgence Publishing, Lutz, FL 33558. www.resurgencepublishing.com.

Bishop James K. Mathews: A Founder Plus

Rev. Clark Lobenstine, Executive Director, The InterFaith Conference

It is a delight to write this paper exploring the significant role which Bishop James K. Mathews had in the founding of the InterFaith Conference (IFC) of Metropolitan Washington, sharing some key learnings and challenges, and reflecting on what such an interreligious organization would look like if it were founded today.

I have described Bishop Mathews as "a founder plus" because he was not only a participant in the beginning of the InterFaith Conference, he carried a vision for what it could become and was one of the initiators of the organization. While visiting Bishop Mathews and his wife, Eunice, in their apartment not long after I arrived in Washington, he asked her to read from a 1974 journal of his that shared his vision. That was four years before the organization was founded! Talk about being a visionary and a founder plus!

I can still hear him telling the story of going to his good friend, Cardinal William Baum, then the head of the Roman Catholic Archdiocese of Washington. "Bill, when we get to the pearly gates, we're going to be asked what we did as religious leaders in the nation's capital. We better have a good answer!"

Bishop Mathews shared his vision for the beginning of what would become the InterFaith Conference with Cardinal Baum and then the two of them went to speak with Episcopal Bishop John T. Walker. They found a very receptive ear, for Bishop Walker had always had a very inclusive understanding of ministry and of his leadership. Indeed, Bishop Walker quickly adopted the vision and made it his own. He had long understood that interfaith work was the pathway to true peace. It was he who called the three summit meetings in the Library of Washington's National Cathedral that led to the formation of the InterFaith Conference. The organizing meeting included Jewish, Protestant and Roman Catholic leaders in March, 1978.

In April of 1978 a major event involving the Muslim community occurred on the day that a group of Protestant judicatory executives were meeting at the Cathedral. They realized that none of them had the personal relationships with Muslim leaders to offer their help -- and they recognized that Muslims needed to be part of the next meeting of the religious leaders to discuss the formation of an interreligious organization in Washington.

Bishop Walker's invitation to the second summit meeting in May included Imam Khalil Abdel Alim of Masjid Muhammad Mosque and Dr. Muhammad Abdul Rauf of the International Islamic Center. Further work over the summer, spearheaded by Bishop Walker's Canon Missioner, the Rev. Canon Lloyd S. Casson, and the Executive Director of the Council of Churches of Greater Washington, Rev. Ernest R. Gibson, led to the final summit meeting in late September, 1978. Gathered around the large oak table in the library of the Cathedral, the religious leaders signed the documents that formed the InterFaith Conference of Metropolitan Washington.

The IFC was the first organization in the world to engage the Islamic, Jewish, Protestant and Roman Catholic faith communities in a metropolitan area devoted to both deepening understanding and building a just community.

In March, 1979, I was invited by the IFC Board of Directors to become the first Executive Director of the InterFaith Conference. The Board was then composed of these religious leaders and a few others. I started working in the IFC office on April 29, 1979.

An early success was holding the first Infant Mortality public hearing in the District of Columbia in May, 1979. The timing of this hearing just two weeks after I arrived was only possible because of the work of the IFC's

Hunger Task Force and its staff before I came. Washington D.C. had the highest infant mortality rate in the country, rivaling that of some third world countries. Choosing to hold the hearings in the chambers of the D.C. City Council added credibility to this effort and reflected relationships that enabled it to happen. But rather than having some 20 persons testify before a group of elected officials, they shared their testimony before a panel of religious leaders, led by the Rev. Canon Lloyd Casson. The major outcome of this testimony was the establishment of the Women, Infant and Children (WIC) program in the District. IFC worked closely with the United Planning Organization and the DC government to bring this widely-respected and Federally funded program to the nation's capital.

An early challenge came only a few months later. The IFC was asked to host an international, interfaith delegation of persons for their day-long visit to Washington. This meeting in Princeton, N.J. with representatives of the world's population by region and by religious identity, was the precursor to the World Conference on Religion and Peace, now known as **Religions for Peace**. Our plan seemed simple enough. We would hold a welcoming ceremony at the Islamic Center, arrange for the delegates to eat lunch with persons of their own faith community in the Washington area, thus assuring an appropriate diet for everyone, and then go to the White House for an afternoon reception with President and Mrs. Carter.

The challenge emerged even as we began. Bishop Walker, our founding President, was to greet the delegates in the courtyard of the Islamic Center. But he became ill that day and could not lead us. So our first Vice-President, Rabbi Eugene Lipman, was asked to do the honors. He kindly agreed. Only then did we learn that this created a major sticking point for our Muslim hosts. Dr. Abdul Rauf, Director of the Islamic Center, was not sure that a rabbi could speak at the Islamic Center! Only with some persuasion were arrangements made to let Rabbi Lipman greet us. I doubt any of our guests ever learned of this early challenge. Today, such an interfaith and collegial occurrence is commonplace.

Some of the Founders' Decisions that Still Guide Us

A number of decisions made in the formation of the InterFaith Conference still guide us. Our founders decided that the IFC would focus both on deepening understanding through interfaith dialogue as well as work actively for justice. This dual mission, as well as the involvement of the Islamic community, made us unique and has been vitally important ever since. Some persons are clearly drawn to us because of one priority or the other, while others realize both are crucial. My friend and colleague, Rev. Bud Heckman, developed a list of some 800 interfaith organizations in the U.S. around the year 2000, either fully volunteer or with staff. The vast majority of them were dialogue centered. Some were issue-driven such as an interfaith coalition on homelessness or hunger. Very few, indeed, understood the need to do both and none had as broad a membership as the IFC was to develop in Washington.

A second guiding principle was that membership was by faith community rather than by individual congregation. Where there was no umbrella body, exceptions were made. For example, there was no umbrella group for the Islamic community at the time of our founding. Three other mosques have joined the Islamic Center and Masjid Muhammad Mosque as members of the IFC. Appropriately there is now the Coordinating Council of Muslim Organizations and there has been some conversation about its becoming a member. If it should become an IFC member, the recommendation has been clearly made that the existing five member mosques remain members to maintain their commitment. The parallel group for the Jewish community is the Jewish Community Relations Council. It is a founding member of the IFC but is much more comprehensive in its membership and scope than the Coordinating Council of Muslim Organizations.

The impact of this second guiding principle was seen, for example, when the Hindu community wanted to join. Actually, the impetus came from one Hindu temple. We responded that membership was by faith community, which led to the formation of the United Hindu and Jain Temples Association. This group now brings together some 14 Hindu temples and one Jain temple. The group continues to thank the InterFaith Conference for our encouragement to form such a body because there is far more collaboration among the temples than before, especially for the annual celebration of Diwali. The Hindu and Jain members have also formed a small committee to respond to requests for speakers from their traditions, facilitating a response to requests we receive from public and private schools, congregations and others.

A third pivotal founding decision was inspired by a challenge coming to the unstaffed interreligious group in Los Angeles. Our founders adopted their principle that groups applying for membership must be "historic." Thus, any religious body that wants to be a part of the InterFaith Conference must be at least 100 years old. This means that they have survived their founder and continued beyond the stage of being a new religious movement.

Some wonder why the Eastern Orthodox Christian community is not a part of the InterFaith Conference. There are several answers to this, but the primary one is that this is their choice. (The same is true for the Unitarian Universalist community in this region.) The Orthodox Christian community participated in the founding meetings of the InterFaith Conference but was divided among their clergy as to whether to join or not. Since membership was by a faith community and not by congregations, that meant they did not join. In fact, our first Constitution and By-Laws stated that if they wanted to join, they would not need to first be Observer Members for a year in recognition of the time already spent with us. Four years later, we met again with the Orthodox Christian Clergy Council (which may have been formed because of their involvement in the founding meetings of the InterFaith Conference). They again made the decision not to join. It should be noted that historically the Orthodox Christian Church has not participated in interfaith relations beyond occasional involvements in Christian-Jewish work.

About 1988, the Church of Jesus Christ of Latter-day Saints joined the InterFaith Conference. It was their first local interfaith involvement in the world. Throughout the development and work of the InterFaith Conference, a significant principle was that each faith community defined itself. So, when the Latter-day Saints wanted to join the IFC, they made clear that they were not only a Christian body, but also that they were neither part of the Protestant nor of the Roman Catholic traditions. Thus when they were admitted, the Protestants and Roman Catholics did not have to make a decision as to whether they were a Christian group or not, which they would have had to do had their membership in IFC been as the Christian faith community. In more recent years, we have been joined by the Baha'i, Buddhist, Sikh and Zoroastrian communities, making the IFC of Metropolitan Washington the most comprehensive organization of its kind in the country. One might say that Bishop Mathews' original vision has been fulfilled.

Some Early Learnings

1. **Building trust is the essential ingredient in our interfaith relationships**: This should come as no surprise, since it is also the glue in friendships. Yet it is vital in interreligious partnerships where our beliefs divide as well as unite us, and where historic differences of race, nationality, language and culture also enter the picture.

2. **Four ways of relating to each other**: Wilfred Cantwell Smith, for years the great teacher of world religions at the Massachusetts Institute of Technology, reflected that there are four ways of relating to each other. We talk about you (usually behind your back); we talk to you (with a sense of superiority that we have the goods and the other person needs them); we talk with you (which is where interfaith dialogue begins), and~~,~~ sometimes~~,~~ we talk with one another introspectively. Building trust happens only at the third and fourth levels of these ways of relating to each other. This model also works in families, congregations, neighborhoods, work places and so on.

3. **How we hold our beliefs is as important as what we believe**: This insight was shared in a Christian-Muslim dialogue group I organized as part of an independent study for my Doctor of Ministry degree from McCormick Seminary. The speaker, a Presbytery executive, referred to research by a gentleman named Rokeach. While I have never found the original research, the finding has guided me. Each of us knows, perhaps by name, persons in their faith tradition who hold their beliefs in tight-fisted and closed-minded ways. We also know others who hold their beliefs in open-handed and open-minded ways. Relationships among

persons of different faiths are far more possible among the second group, whatever the specific beliefs are. Thus, whether I would describe my beliefs as fundamentalist, conservative, moderate, liberal or radical, (we might place these positions along a horizontal line) if I hold them in an open way, and if I find satisfaction in discussing them with persons with different views (an approach that puts one somewhere above the median on a vertical axis), then dialogue is not only possible, it is likely to be very fruitful.

4. **"I need the other to understand myself:"** This insight by a Jewish participant in a multi-religious dialogue helps us better understand what can happen in an interfaith exchange or even between two members of the same congregation. We may find the other person asking us questions that appear to be naïve. Don't be surprised by that. Instead, use it as an invitation to grow, because the naïve question probably reflects that the language you are using does not communicate to the other. If a Sikh shares a concept I am not familiar with in Gurumuki, or a Muslim does the same in Arabic, or a Jew in Hebrew, my question can lead my partner in dialogue to expand his or her understanding of that phrase by having to explain it. The same can certainly also be true if both partners are speaking in English. The "code words" of our own tradition are numerous and often they are not explained or discussed within our tradition because we have grown up with them, because everyone assumes you know what they mean, too. Christian words or phrases such as "being washed in the blood of the lamb," or "trinity" or "communion" may be central to one's beliefs but may not communicate accurately -- or at all -- to someone from another tradition.

5. Another learning seems simple enough, but one may need to remind others of it. **Start with what we share in common before we get to areas of disagreement**. In the 1980s I received a telephone call from a campus minister at a local university. He was excited that for the first time on his campus the Jewish, Muslim and Christian student associations wanted to meet together and they wanted to talk about the Middle East. Would I come to facilitate this dialogue? I told him I would be glad to come but I was not going to start with the Middle East! I wanted to start with what we shared in common. It was, thereby, a successful event.

6. **There are more and more wonderful resources to use**: When the InterFaith Conference began in 1978, little was available to guide us. For example, we developed our own Guidelines for Interfaith Prayer Services and Guidelines for Interfaith Dialogue. They seem fairly basic now, but some groups are still finding them helpful. For years we have used and sold copies of the Multifaith Calendar prepared by our colleagues in Vancouver, Canada. Now much of the same information is available on line at www.interfaithcalendar.org. Being a Perfect Stranger is a widely used book to help persons invited for the first time to a *bar mitzvah* or to a Sikh wedding or to a Christian church service knowing what to do, what to wear, what to bring (if anything), etc.

7. **Find and use sources that are primary for you, even though others in your tradition may understand them very differently**: I have preached and taught, for example, on this injunction from the first letter of Peter, Chap. 3, v. 15: "Always be prepared to give an account of the hope that is within you, but do so with gentleness and reverence." What a difference it would make if we all could not only articulate the hope that is within us, but also share it with gentleness and reverence!

8. **Some people want to emphasize we all really believe the same thing**: This was brought home to me as I met with a group of Muslim scholars from abroad. One of the imams said we all really believe the same thing. It happened to be Good Friday and I was leaving my morning session with them to go to a church service nearby. I replied that it is out of the Muslim love of Jesus and belief in his being a prophet, a nebi, that the Qur'an says that one who looked like Jesus was crucified on the cross. The Bible teaches me differently, and I was going to this Good Friday noon service to remember that Jesus did die on a cross and why.

9. **Be as eager to learn from another as to share with the other:** How differently our relations with neighbors and friends of other faiths would be if we remembered this. As a Christian who is part of the majority faith in this country, it is especially important to learn from others first.

10. **Distinguish what is central in your religious beliefs and what is cultural**: I remember reading the story of a Russian Jewish émigré to this

country who had never heard of Hanukkah. Now Hanukkah does have important religious roots. But its prominence in this country is directly related to our culture's emphasis on Christmas, stimulated by commercial interests. It is actually a minor Jewish holiday. The Christmas tree would be another such example. There is no reference to it in the Bible or in the earliest Christian church. Yet you'd be hard pressed to find a Christian home or church without one these days. A third example I learned years later after a Muslim staff member died of cancer, is about the Egyptian tradition of having a memorial service for someone 40 days after that person dies. The imam who was glad to lead it made clear it was not an Islamic tradition but an Egyptian cultural tradition.

Examples of Collaborative Work to Build a Just Society

We are the InterFaith Conference of Metropolitan Washington. Bishop Mathews and our other founders were clear that we should bring together regional religious leaders to address regional moral and social problems, but that we should not become a direct service organization ourselves. In our first ten years we frequently played the role of what I have termed "the neutral but committed partner." This was especially true in establishing the Coalition for the Homeless. A couple of leaders in organizations working with the homeless approached us about developing a coalition of such service providers. "We don't have enough trust with each other to do this," one of them told me. Two part-time staff persons were hired for the preparatory work that took a number of months. One surveyed some 60 different service providers to learn what they saw as gaps in services and duplicative services and to gauge their interest in forming a coalition. The other person worked on the details of holding a day-long meeting which we hoped would lead to a shared commitment to form such a coalition. After a successful founding conference, I worked with an intern for about a year to develop the Coalition for the Homeless until it could be spun off as a separate 501(c)3 organization, and it continues today to function as a prominent entity in our region.

We likewise played a central role, after holding the first public hearing on infant mortality, in bringing into being the Women, Infant and Children

(WIC) program for the District of Columbia. This was done in partnership with the United Planning Organization, the CAP agency for D.C. that had been formed in the 1960s and received significant anti-poverty funding from the Federal government. We also developed the Capital Area Community Food Bank which now distributes some 20,000,000 pounds of food a year to over 700 member agencies throughout the metropolitan area.

Similar developmental work was done to start GROW, Garden Resources of Washington, which focused on helping neighbors create gardens of vegetables and flowers out of trash-strewn lots. The program also strengthened nourishment at the same time. We developed a physician's network of specialists who would receive *pro bono* referrals from one of the nonprofit clinics on an agreed-upon schedule (e.g., once a week; once a month, etc.) After the specialist had seen the patient, the clinic did the necessary follow-up work. After a couple of years, this was merged with the Archdiocesan Physicians' Network and its work continues today.

All of this work could not have been done without an active IFC Hunger Task Force which had at least one staff person throughout our first ten years, and which received national denominational funding when such money was much more available than it is now. I remember calling a national church office that had just sent us a check for $10,000 for this work. I told them that I had planned a decrease in their support over three years and had sent them a proposal requesting $7,500 for year two. The person in charge told me that we were doing a good job and to keep the $10,000. He noted that they had budgeted that amount for three years and so we would be receiving the same amount the following two years! That never happens today.

In the mid-to-late 1980s AIDS and HIV-Positive test results were just beginning to get the community's attention. Only two religious groups existed which dealt with this, and one of them was not recognized by its faith community. Our work on this critical health issue enabled the religious community to respond in meaningful ways and encouraged our member traditions to start their own task forces on AIDS. Developing the first interfaith pastoral reflection on AIDS, apparently the first in the world and certainly in the U.S., took six months of finding common ground between a task force of religiously-based activists and our Board of Directors which was asking many questions. Once approved, we followed it with public policy recommendations. We developed 1,000 packets of educational material which were distributed throughout the religious community and we then held the first interfaith training opportunities in the world for those working with caregivers of persons with AIDS.

It was only years later that someone told me that when the U.S. House of Representatives was getting ready to vote on the Ryan White bill to provide funding to organizations serving those with AIDS, when a member got up to oppose the bill saying AIDS was the wrath of God. Another member, holding up our IFC policy statement on AIDS, said it definitely was not the wrath of God and here were six historic faith communities saying so! (Our statement actually took no position on if/how AIDS was related to God, but the member's holding up our policy statement was an unexpected affirmation of the impact we were having!)

More recently, our Steering Committee for the InterFaith Center for Advancing Justice has focused on religious freedom issues. For example, when the Soka Gakkai International (SGI) Buddhist community in Washington wanted to build its "cultural center" on Embassy Row, some neighbors asked the D.C. Board of Zoning Adjustments to deny its application to build this building as a matter of right (since it was a congregation) and instead to make it seek a much more difficult-to-get exemption. Our statements to the head of the Board of Zoning Adjustments (BZA) that this was a legitimate group, an active partner of the Washington Area Buddhist Network, and a member of the InterFaith Conference. What they called a cultural center was really a house of worship with many similar features to a church, and it was crucial to the BZA's approval of the permit which allowed the SGI group to build as a matter of right.

In the November, 2009 meeting of the IFC Board of Directors, members approved a statement which I had drafted in response to the killings a few days before at Fort Hood in Texas. This reflected an important witness of the InterFaith Conference over the years – standing with a community when it was attacked. It gave the imprimatur of our now eleven member faith communities to the condemnation of this attack, which many Muslim organizations and mosques had already done.

In early December of 2008 and 2009, we led special interfaith programs that were co-sponsored by the Washington Center of the Soka Gakkai International (SGI) and by the U.N. Association for the National Capital Region. Both were hosted by SGI as well. The first focused on the sixtieth anniversary of the U.N. Declaration of Human Rights. The printed program included one-page statements from ten of our member faith communities on why they supported the U.N. Declaration. Their representatives spoke very briefly in the actual program, with summary statements prepared for them from their written statements. This format effectively demonstrated interfaith support for the U.N. Declaration of Human Rights. It also took a lot of staff time from our very part-time Consultant for Religious Freedom to gather these one-page statements for our member faith communities.

So when the Board agreed to host a special service for the U.N. Day for Persons with Disabilities in early December, 2009, in the midst of serious fiscal constraints in our budget, the Board did so with the caveat that much less time of our Consultant would be used. The excellent program was made possible by greater involvement by the members of the InterFaith Justice Center's Steering Committee. It included three persons sharing reflections on the U.N. Day from the Jewish, Protestant and Buddhist faith communities.

Handling Divisive Issues

I am periodically asked how the IFC handles divisive issues. The answer is several-fold. The first lesson that I shared – the key role of trust in interfaith relationships – is one answer. Part of the way I have done this is by working quietly behind the scenes and rarely seeking publicity. For example, when Pope Benedict XVI made his remarks at Regenstuck University which created such a stir in the Islamic and wider world, I was easily and quickly able to use established relationships to bring together the Papal Nuncio (the Pope's Representative to the United States) with five key local and national Muslims for a two-hour, off-the-record dialogue about the ramifications of the incident. Both sides agreed the meeting was very useful. In keeping with the nature of the meeting (and my own style), I turned down a request from one of the Muslim participants that his organization arrange a news conference afterwards.

A second answer is that we generally vote by consensus and stay quite focused on the national capital region. Troublesome issues such as the Middle East or controversies elsewhere in the States are generally not dealt with. The few exceptions, such as the Board's statement on the Fort Hood incident, are usually related to the denigration of a whole faith community by the actions of one or a few of its members.

A third answer is that we have used the difficult issue process of the National Coalition Building Institute (NCBI). This was very useful for us on the issues raised by the leadership of Minister Farrakhan of the Million Man March and on the issues raised by prayer in public schools. The difficult issue process focuses on listening well enough to the opposing member's answers to be able to say them back to the first person's satisfaction, and then asks each representative of the two opposing sides to share a story of why they felt the way they did. The final step is to ask what areas of common ground could the persons with opposite views find on which they could work together.

A fourth answer is to find our common ground in the midst of the divisions. For example, recently the Archdiocese of Washington was strongly opposed to a bill that would recognize the right of all persons in D.C. to get married, including gay and lesbian couples, while some other member religious traditions strongly supported the bill. In fact there was a significant group of clergy that mobilized for the bill. I testified on behalf of the IFC, explaining why I was not taking a stand on the bill, but was emphasizing the need for civility in the debate of this issue as well as offering to mediate among reasonable persons with opposing views.

Deepening Understanding

Unlike a great many interfaith groups that focus only on deepening understanding through interfaith dialogue, we have found that the trust and understanding built in this process often motivates us to act together. At the same time, when we are acting together, we are also asking ourselves why we do this and that generates more dialogue.

Bishop James K. Mathews: A Founder Plus

Deeping understanding is one of the two legs we stand on. As I have often said, it is a whole lot easier to get around on two legs than to have only one. I am so grateful to our founders for their clarity that we must both deepen understanding and build a just community!

Interfaith dialogue has occurred in many ways within the InterFaith Conference over our first thirty years. From the beginning, dialogues have been a part of almost every single Board or Assembly meeting. (Our Assembly is our larger stakeholders' group that meets three times a year and of which Board members are also a part.)

For years we had a Commission for Dialogue which planned Spring Public Dialogues. They were the region's largest opportunities for persons of diverse faiths (or no faith) to come together to share and learn together about an issue. Now our InterFaith Center for Building Community is focused on this responsibility.

We also work with congregations and judicatories to strengthen the understanding of diverse faiths and of interfaith relations among their members. We are working now with a local synagogue which will host an interfaith dialogue on understandings of God. We are also working now with a local church on a conference it will have among Christians, Jews and Muslims and how people of faith use the resources of their traditions to respond in a situation provoking fear. That could be another terrorist attack, a flu pandemic, a weather-related incident or something else.

Where possible, the InterFaith Conference has helped congregations and others approach a topic they have chosen from a multireligious perspective and not just from an Abrahamic perspective. We also recognize, however, that for many, this Abrahamic focus is their priority.

For example, for three years we resourced a dinner dialogue held by the Commission on Unity and Interreligious Concerns during the annual meeting of the Baltimore-Washington Conference of the United Methodist Church. Eighty to 100 persons came each year from many different congregations. Twice I moderated a panel of Jewish, Christian and Muslim speakers and once I led a panel of persons from eastern religious traditions.

Interfaith prayer services are another way in which we express our unity in diversity and deepen understanding of our many traditions by those attending. The IFC has for more than twenty years coordinated the region's only multireligious service for Dr. Martin Luther King's birthday. On Sunday afternoon, January 10, 2010, the service will be hosted again at the historic African American Asbury United Methodist Church. We are delighted that Dr. Dennis Wiley, co-pastor of the Covenant Baptist Church and an expert on the theology of Dr. Howard Thurman, and Rabbi Harold White, who studied under Rabbi Abraham Heschel for five years, will reflect on these giants' contributions to the mission and ministry of Dr. King.

Among our many other interfaith prayer services, another that stands out is the service we held on the morning of September 13, 2001, two days after the terrorist attacks on the Pentagon and the World Trade Center. I spent September 12 crafting the service and engaging seventeen faith community leaders to participate. The service brought nearly 700 persons together to express our anguish, pray for justice and share our hopes in the midst of this crisis. As it turned out, the service also introduced Cardinal Theodore McCarrick, who had recently been installed as the leader of the Archdiocese of Washington, to many of his fellow religious leaders and deeply impressed him about the InterFaith Conference as well.

A New Vision to Help us Better Implement Our Mission

I have mentioned our InterFaith Center for Advancing Justice and the InterFaith Center for Building Community. There is also a third, the InterFaith Center for Nurturing Understanding, which oversees our work with children and youth. The new vision adopted by our Board in the fall of 2006 followed three summer meetings of a dozen key members of the Board, visualized these three centers as three overlapping circles. This design was meant to emphasize that while each Center has its own responsibilities, each also interacts with and has shared responsibilities with the other two Centers. The Vision articulates a high visible "signature" project for each Center, as well as two internal priorities and a collaborative project with another Center.

The Vision is, of necessity, also a flexible one. One Center's signature project has been replaced by another one and that has been revised again. As fiscal constraints have forced us to work with a bare-bones staff and as many Board members are taking on additional responsibilities, the Vision may need to be refined further. A Board retreat in January 2010 will be discussing what two key projects with fund-raising experience or potential will be the priorities of each Center.

Challenges Now

We have fiscal challenges similar to those facing most nonprofit organizations as well as congregations and many businesses. Our fiscal challenge at this time of course reflects the economic situation of our nation and world. But it also reflects the fact that we have emphasized fund-raising events over the years much more than building a base of on-going giving by donors, small and large.

This now requires greater attention and is the focus of our new "Friends of the IFC" thrust, seeking monthly donors as well as more individuals who are contributing on a one-time or annual basis. Related to this is the further development of our direct connections with congregations while our membership is primarily with judicatories and faith communities.

A second challenge is greater use of our website, www.ifcmw.org, to make our programs and work more accessible as we also "go green."

A third challenge may be our present location. Although a godsend in many ways, we are not as accessible by public transportation as we used to be. While in the summer of 2009 we had nine interns working with us --our most ever--in the fall of 2009 we only had one. A number of other interns, very interested in our work, turned us down and told us it was because of not being very accessible by public transportation.

A fourth challenge is the opportunity of growing partnerships and sharing our office with other small organizations. Figuring out what services we can offer (such as accounting) is key to developing the agreements with one or more other small nonprofits.

A fifth challenge is expanding the use of the resources we offer. For example, seven area public school systems are using our Teaching About

Religion supplementary textbook for high school teachers of world religions, world history and social studies. But we need to develop the connections that would engage a couple of important public school districts in our region. And what of private and parochial schools using it? Few congregations have discovered it, but it would be a wonderful resource for adult and youth education programs there.

A final challenge I would articulate is that of engaging the next generation of leaders for interfaith work. Bishop Mathews and others founded the InterFaith Conference. I and others are providing leadership now. But what will happen in five or ten or fifteen years? Engaging the next generation of leaders is one of our intentions by encouraging college and graduate students to intern with us. So this was our part of the reason for previously having a strong program for high school youth and for recently engaging children through our InterFaith Children's Theatre Company.

What Would It Take Now to Create an InterFaith Conference?

If Bishop Mathews were building an InterFaith Conference now, what would he have to do? I would say that starting the group with a dual mission of deepened understanding and building a just community is key. Adding a third leg of community service and funds to pay interns would make the new organization even stronger.

Because he would be developing this new group in a much more difficult economic climate, it would be doubly important to get a strong "buy-in" from the groups one wanted to engage as members. This is made all the more difficult by the shrinking budgets of area judicatories and faith communities.

A third challenge would be how to get this "buy-in." Does one work with the "bishop-types" of each tradition one wants to become a member of the new organization? Does one seek the "buy-in" from their active compatriots who will get the "yes" from their bishops? IFC began by doing the first and this was key to starting our organization. But after two or three years, the religious leaders of our diverse traditions passed the mantle of leadership to their deputies, and in this way it was clear the InterFaith Conference was moving forward.

However one resolves the previous dilemma, one must still keep the key religious leaders involved. The IFC has chosen to do this by involving them several times a year in our “Faith Group Leaders” meetings but the efficacy of that is being questioned as attendance has shrunk.

Would a new interfaith organization being formed today use the same representative structure of the InterFaith Conference, where each member faith community has constitutionally reserved seats on the Board of Directors? These persons are selected by their faith communities and elected by the InterFaith Conference. Also, the Board is not a fund-raising group, although its role in development is being encouraged. Or should it be designed differently? There are strengths and weaknesses in the current structure and these would have to be evaluated if a new interreligious group were being formed today.

I would encourage the new organization to be formed from the beginning of diverse religious traditions, not just Abrahamic ones. But I also think that the insight of our founders is key as well – engage “historic religious traditions.” I’m sure some of our members would leave us now, or would not have joined us in the first place, if groups such as the Wiccans or Scientology were at the table.

Closing

Thank you again for the privilege of sharing these learnings from 30 years of my leadership of the InterFaith Conference of Metropolitan Washington. This organization would not have developed without the vision of Bishop James K. Mathews, nor without the piloting in our formation by Bishop John T. Walker. Their staff and others played key roles as well that must not be forgotten.

Spirit of the EcoRestorative Movement:
Beyond Sustainability - An Evolutionary Process - Toward Care for the Greater Community of Life

Tim Watson, NCARB, Principal, TLW Architect, Hillsborough, N.C.

Preamble to the International Earth Charter

We stand at a critical moment in earth's history, a time when humanity must choose its future.

As the world becomes increasingly interdependent and fragile, the future at once holds great peril and great promise. To move forward we must recognize that in the midst of a magnificent diversity of cultures and life forms, we are one human family and one Earth community with a common destiny. We must join together to bring forth a sustainable global society founded on respect for nature, universal human rights, economic justice, and a culture of peace. Towards this end, it is imperative that we, the peoples of Earth, declare our responsibility to one another, to the greater community of life, and to future generations.

Prologue – "Spirit of the EcoRestorative Movement"

> *And God blessed them, and said unto them, "Be fruitful, and multiply, and replenish the earth, and subdue it, and have dominion over the fish of the sea, and over the fowl of the air, and over every living thing that moveth upon the earth." (Gen. 1:28)*

Personal Introduction and the Mathews Legacy

While pushing wheelbarrows on the reclamation project known as Fifth City on Chicago's West side, fascination for designing buildings first stirred my early adult life. Working at the former Institute of Cultural Affairs seminary campus found me hauling old row house construction debris during the hottest days of 1963. I remember our talks in the shade of the old seminary dining hall. We brainstormed about how bricks and mortar would set the stage for reshaping human community. But what I didn't know about then: using bricks and mortar also changes the natural world, for better or worse.

Before that time in Chicago, life around my Uncle Joe, Aunt Lynn (I really miss her), and the Mathews boys in Texas, drew my attention to the idea that I, too, could serve humanity. In Austin, the Ecumenical Institute's pilot "Religious Studies One" (RS-1) workshop confounded me. In those days I had no idea how this extraordinary experience was to shape my journey into life's Great Mystery. The underlying spirit of the Mathews family certainly includes our dear Bishop Jim's (Ken to our family) contributions to my life. On numerous occasions he gave me his counsel, his time and his abiding inspiration. All this nudged me forward. This family legacy has helped form a man who sees himself as a member of the global village, and a man who passionately serves humanity in his own way forward.

"Building the Earth"!

Ensuing studies at Rice University birthed in me a reverent regard for Ian McHarg's ideas, who authored his landmark book Design with Nature in 1969. Ian's ideas sparked our graduate class toward the integration of human activity and care for the natural environment. Such ideas caused me to rethink how best to apply my Master of Urban Design degree through the application of sustainable, ecologically responsible design.

In June 1993 I again found myself back in Chicago. There, while participating in launching the first international architectural convention, we formulated a global "Declaration of Interdependence for a Sustainable Future." My life and architectural practice was transformed. Since that time I have sought out a way to "build the Earth" through the use of sustainable design ideas. The seeds of the ecorestorative design ideas I will offer today germinated in Chicago. Since those times I have been blessed with the help and inspiration of many fellow Earth stewards.

The insights gained in those earlier years blossomed when I read Father Thomas Berry's The Dream of the Earth. His visionary grasp of humanity's relationship with Earth helped me see how human perception about the natural world is fundamentally shaping our time in history with the passing of each day. He foresaw our rush toward a new era wherein the natural world will seem to have turned the tables against us. He envisioned the natural world regaining the reverent attention once deemed so worthy by our ancestors. He also understood the human community would finally have to come to grips with the visceral prospect of its own extinction.

This inheritance of family, education, and inspiration, finds me grateful for our shared Mathews legacy. This legacy has helped prepare me to be an eager participant in this symposium. It is a lifelong honor to stand amongst the ranks of those attending this gathering with the intention of "transforming the legacy" Brother Joe and Bishop Jim have so ably entrusted to us.

Overview – Our challenge for the 21st century

Nine years ago representatives from 175 nation states, including the United States, concluded in the preamble to the international Earth Charter:

> "We stand at a critical moment in earth's history,
> a time when humanity must choose its future."

How transformative can this simple line be in our lives, at this Symposium?

Before beginning, let each one of us first consider our sense of commitment to this preamble. Let us collectively determine a course of action on this day that acknowledges:

"Our greatest challenge of the 21st century is to allow all future generations the right to life, and the right to participate in life processes equal in quality to that of our own time."

Transformation cannot take place without the heat of human spirit. We attending this Symposium are living at a watershed time. If we choose to draw upon this well of human spirit, we are drawing upon this Symposium's greatest gift. We do so knowing that it is this spirit that will ultimately shape the outcome of our greatest challenge of the 21st century. So when I speak about the evolutionary process taking us beyond sustainable thinking towards eco-spiritual thinking, this is what I am talking about.

On October 24, 2009 people in 181 countries came together for the most widespread day of environmental action in the planet's history. This grassroots inspired event is simply known as "350." Millions across the world are aware that the Earth's CO^2 count has exceeded the scientific community's recommended threshold of 350 parts per million. People in all walks of life and different faiths are calling for action because they have come to believe the climate crisis is being affected by increasing levels of CO^2. Here is clear evidence for us all to witness. Humankind is capable of taking action locally and transforming political agendas globally. Because of this event, the world is a different place today. Through witnessing the 350 event, we see the power of human spirit at its best.

Global warming is heating up the sustainability movement. Some say the green revolution is being driven by climate change. What we see in these two terms is an evolution of thought. Today sustainable concepts have taken the architectural design profession beyond the boundaries of its previous notions about "green architecture." What we are to consider here is a look down the road toward future architectural and urban design. Down that road we will encounter ecorestorative design.

The idea of ecorestorative design and its attention to the greater community of life is tied to climate change, and to life itself. More important to this Symposium, and to the Wesley Theological Seminary's (WTS) dedication to help sustain the Mathews legacy, is how we each can play a role in restoring the Earth to its indigenous level of fecundity. That is to say, let us commit to a course of action that will help regain the capacity of life to flourish on this planet. It is a daunting challenge. If it is not met, the scientific community generally agrees the survival of countless species, as well as our own, is at risk.

> "Climate change is a reality. Life depends on a sustainable environment. With no world, there can only be nothing--no birds, no animals, no trees, no us. That's why getting involved in 350.org is so important--it's an effective way to take action to turn around the climate crisis." – Archbishop Desmond Tutu

From Moscow to "Transforming the Legacy"

Toward the end of his stellar career of service to the scientific and educational communities, Dr. Carl Sagan traveled with 22 globally renowned scientists to Moscow in 1990. There representatives from 83 countries attended the Global Forum of Spiritual and Parliamentary Leaders on Human Survival. Their statement listed the dangers of global warming, the depletion of food resources, the extinction of plant and animal species, and the destruction of rain forests, among other topics. According to the *New York Times* report, this Global Forum determined:

> "Problems of such magnitude, and solutions demanding so broad a perspective, must be recognized from the outset as having a religious as well as a scientific dimension."

It is within this context we consider the challenge being placed before this Symposium. This is a time crying for new ways of thinking, and for bold action. It is a story crying out for human reconnection to our sacred bond with Earth. It is a story yearning for a sense of empowerment, a sense of direction and clear purpose. Today I believe that sense of direction and purpose is within reach. Through its nurturing of the human spirit, the faith community can determine to mobilize its clergy and laity towards fomenting new forms of urban revitalization and educational concordance.

Of all the environments to be found on Earth, the most diversified human cultural environments are to be found in cities. Contrasting this, urbanized land is in most dire need of reclamation, soil rejuvenation, and natural ecosystems restoration. Cities comprise man-made environments severely disconnected from natural processes.

The combination of disenfranchised people and cities in ecological distress sets the stage for the coming "Re-greening of America" revolution. It is time to step upon that green stage to champion the future needs of millions of people. The faith community is in a strong position to influence policy through practical demonstrations. Aided by the faith community's example, the youth of inner city America can see for themselves the promise of a new green world beckoning their enthusiastic participation. The Re-greening America approach is about applying appropriate technologies to render our streets, vacant lots, and roof tops as contributors to the restoration of our planet's ecosystem. In so doing, Wesley Theological Seminary can help rekindle the sanctity of Earth in millions of people's hearts.

The Ecumenical Institute in Fifth City proved it is possible to do the impossible. There Joe Mathews and his colleagues, with support from afar by Bishop Mathews, made their stand. In the end, Chicago's West side was transformed. We too can resolve to take on the greatest challenge of the century: to test and launch the Re-greening of America campaign in the toughest arena – urban America. Cities are the beachheads of the future. They are our best hope.

Across America and throughout the world, thousands of faith leadership members are convening and communicating with each other. They are awakening to the global consensus taking form about global warming. Let us work with them to transform the legacy of Joseph Wesley and James Kenneth Mathews in ways totally new to all of us. Let us march with them as we embrace a humane doctrine for all earth's life communities.

> "Anything else you're interested in is not going to happen if you can't breathe the air and drink the water. Don't sit this one out. Do something."
>
> Carl Sagan

The Great Shift

What is driving the great shift from an anthropocentrically-dominated world toward a perceived interdependent and humane relationship between people and the natural world?

Most of us are aware of the previously mentioned challenges and their attendant social and economic inequities. These challenges belie the decline of Earth's natural bio-capacity upon which humankind ultimately depends. The human community now consumes 40 percent of all currently available food-based energy resources on Earth. That is to say that within the *aegis* of horticultural and naturally occurring biomass processes, humanity is consuming almost half of what is available to all species of life. This onslaught is accelerating in the face of a shrinking global biomass dinner table. For example, recently global food reserves sank to a 61-day supply – an all-time low. Information from the National Academy of Sciences shows us this:

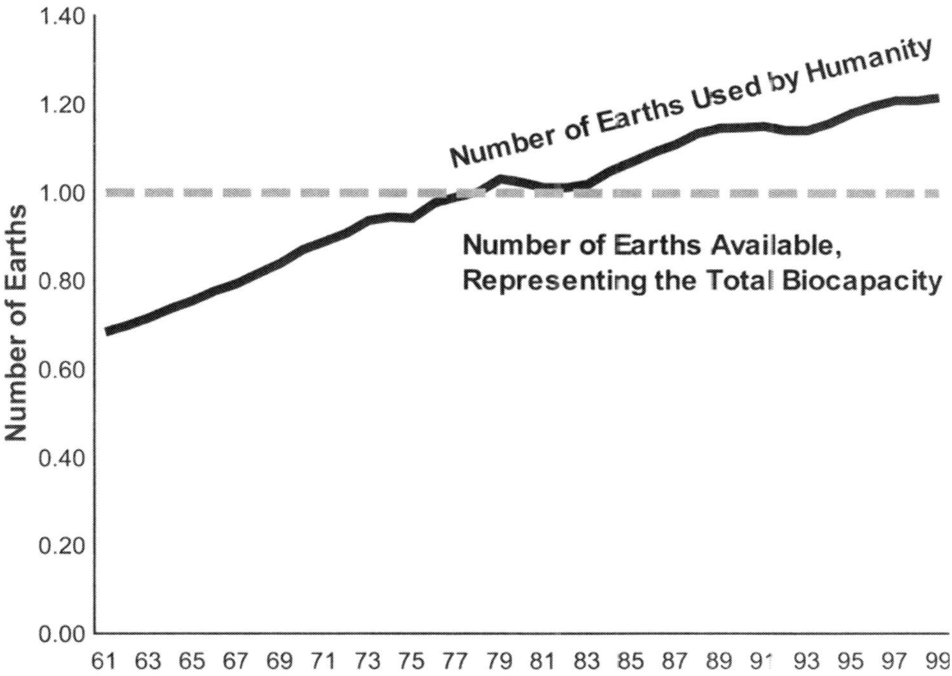

This overdrawing and erosion of our planet's capacity to support life is pressing the human community to adopt measures intended to slow, and ultimately overcome, the growing decline of Earth's carrying capacity. The weight of human intervention into the natural world is compelling us to convene, to reassess, to pay attention – however inconvenient or economically compromising sustainable-use policies might seem.

Even in the architectural world, a shift from anthropocentric bottom line ethics toward addressing the larger Earth community is taking place. As far back as 1992, *The Hannover Principles* were developed as foundational guidelines for ecological design. One of the key principles listed for dissemination at the 2000 Hannover World Fair:

"Respect relationships between spirit and matter."

This acknowledgement of spirit living in and being expressed through the physical world marks the emergence of a great shift in perception in industrial/technological societies.

The Hannover Principles helped usher in a New Earth Story compelling us to consider joining forces with all life communities. In so doing they embraced the worlds of spirit and matter as being integral with one another. Here we see people representing building sciences and design services willing to acknowledge the presence of Spirit as an integral part of the ecological design process!

Technological Mindset - Our Last Great Hope?

Central to the challenges of our time resides western culture's last great hope: technology.

Many people living in industrialized societies are accustomed to believe science will continue to pull the proverbial "white rabbit out of the hat." Our insistence on individual freedom and our inherited pride in seeing technology as the instrument for the control of nature underlies our wish to continue our reliance on technology to avoid catastrophe. We continue to think in terms of inventing new technologies that will enable us to produce more food, more inventions, and more clever fixes. So far it has not worked.

Consumerism, global investment practices, social inequity, and slow progression towards emancipation of gender, of poverty, and of human rights have played a role in leading us toward environmental meltdown. If developing countries were to adopt America's level of consumerism, it would take almost six planet Earth's to match the western world's narcissistic appetite (see above National Academy of Sciences graph).

However, in the midst of our love affair with technology, enough danger signals have occurred to cause a growing number of us to reconsider the march down this road.

For example, according to the World Wide Fund for Nature, glacier melt is now predicted to severely affect the lives of two billion people when the Himalayas' glaciers disappear within the next thirty-five years (see Appendix). One of many global warming implications resulting from Greenland's alarming ice melt (scientists are saying it is melting much faster than previously believed) will see Bangladesh inundated with sea rise level covering almost half its land area. Whole Micronesian populations are at risk. Lower lying coastal areas, particularly in Louisiana, Florida, and the North Carolina outer banks will be affected in the United States. The scientific community has reached consensus on human generated CO^2 accelerating the global warming process. Within the context of the global community, we are faced with the moral question of participating in this impending tragic ending of so many human lives.

Let us take a look at a sampling of our last great hope: new technologies which many people believe will eventually help turn the global warming tide.

-- Thin film and applied photovoltaic coatings which can transform roofing and building siding into solar energy collectors.

-- "Phase change" adjuncts to traditional wall and ceiling insulation products which reduce ranges of temperature variations in buildings.

-- Precast concrete foundation cisterns that are designed to store rainwater, structurally support buildings, and add malleable thermal mass to buildings.

-- Biodegradable packaging materials and related products which can be used as natural fertilizer inputs in China.

-- Recycled and reused materials in manufacturing can be seen in Ford's demonstration "Model U" automotive design process, which eliminates waste streams coming from manufacturing. It demonstrates a recycling process generally known as "biotechnological food resources."

-- LED lighting luminaries which use a fraction of the energy used by fluorescent lamps (fluorescent technology uses mercury and therefore is a waste hazard).

-- Aerophonic crop rooftop production is being developed in Pacific Rim countries with the objective of creating urban farming industries on top of buildings having flat roofs (presages use of urbanized areas as food resources for people).

-- Renewable fuel resources intended to serve reciprocating engine technology will move from use of precious food stocks (like corn) to algae propagation which can generate doubled biomass production every 24 hours.

-- Fusion energy production may become available within the next twenty years (this timeframe is too far into the future to significantly affect CO^2 emission reductions needed to neutralize greenhouse gas propagation in time).

Another landmark development is the new "high performance" building certification process now being used in the United States. Governmental and educational facilities are adopting the use of a new building design and construction certification process known as Leadership in Energy and Environmental Design (LEED). Architects and people associated with the design services industry are using LEED guidelines to help them develop sustainable buildings and related site improvements. The incorporation of these sustainable design criteria is intended to reduce energy and resource consumption, which in turn helps reduce CO^2 emissions.

All these are wonderful developments. But they are not enough.

Within the next ten to twenty years, "LEED – New Construction" buildings will comprise less than 2 percent of America's building stock. What about all the existing structures whose thermal performance pales in comparison to these high performance buildings? And what about the economics involved in retrofitting the new technologies listed above? Using LEED guidelines will take more time than is left for us to transform our inventory of extractive use buildings into net energy exporting buildings. In the face of this situation, what can be done to bring America in line with average worldwide energy use patterns?

Photovoltaics, solar water heating arrays, wind generated electricity, and associated renewable energy technologies are promising a better tomorrow in the minds of most people. Such technological applications are very important to our future. They are indeed part of the solution to global warming. However at this time in history they pose an important drawback. These sophisticated delivery systems require a high degree of specialization, centralized distribution patterns, and highly skilled labor resources to produce, install, and maintain them. There is limited access to such technologies. When conceived in so-called third world nations, they can be seen as "hard technology." They can be viewed as such because they are difficult to acquire and bring on-line in most underdeveloped locations around the world. What is needed to counterbalance the need for these hard technologies are sustainable scientifically based globally applicable processes which can be referred to as "soft technologies."

Soft Technologies – Our New Partner

Resolution of climate change is a global enterprise. This challenge will command the attention and participation of every empowered man, woman, and child on the planet. The application of hard technology is, unfortunately, reserved for the fortunate few who have access to deep-pocketed economic and highly specialized industrialized resources. Enter "soft technologies."

"Soft technology" is about using locally available human and physical resources as we find them. It is about applying a combination of ancient and contemporary sciences. This "soft tech" process draws upon what may be termed Agrarian Earth Science.

The use of Agrarian Earth Science was popularized in the western world by a man named Bill Mollison in the 1980s. He and his partner in Australia developed nature-based ways for people to interact with surrounding ecosystems. Part of his inspiration drew upon ancient technologies developed by indigenous peoples. Mollison saw it was possible for humans to live in harmony with nature. He coined the word "permaculture" to identify this contemporary cultural form of living lightly on the land. Today one can find examples of whole communities whose interactions with nature are based on "permaculture," "Natureco," and related Agrarian Earth Sciences throughout the world.

Soft technologies involve processes that are decentralized and available to people everywhere in the world. Such technologies combine ancient agrarian sciences with contemporary Agrarian Earth Science. Through the test of at least forty countries these processes have proven to be truly sustainable. Numerous examples involving the application of soft technologies can be found wherein entire communities of people participate in their long-term horticultural operations.

Today similar Agrarian Earth Science based modalities are needed to complement the use of hard technologies. Perhaps the greatest advantage of this blending of old and new has to do with the fact that unskilled human resources can be called upon to put Agrarian Earth Science to use. Contrasting the use of "hard tech" which is costly and inaccessible to many people throughout the world, application of "permaculture" based sustainable crop production can be universally adopted.

Here is the unaddressed opportunity of our time: combinations of hard and soft technologies can be used in cities and human habitations throughout the world to address climate change.

As previously stated, cities are our beachhead landing ground. The combined use of these technologies will permit people from all walks of life to participate, whatever their education and socio-economic background.

Universal human participation is key to meaningful global ecological transformation. The environmental challenges of our time can be successfully met; however, not by the few and not alone by those whose resources seem up to the challenge. As was the case on December 7, 1941, almost every able-bodied adult in America and in other countries joined forces to "do their bit" to win the war. So, too, we must enlist and galvanize all members of our society to participate in winning this greatest global challenge in mankind's history. This combination of hard and soft technologies is the means whereby every engaged person can "do their bit."

Innovative Visions for the Future

Nowhere in the world of human-built environment has there been a greater need to embrace these new ideas than in cities. Nowhere in the world are there more opportunities to adopt and apply ecorestorative processes than in cities.

<u>Local economic flows</u>: This process begins with people and the decentralized economic activity patterns they can generate. The key barometer for local exchange and flow of commerce is money distributed within local neighborhoods and communities like Fifth City in Chicago. When compared to the energy-intensive centralized corporate world, such economies are less energy consumptive and, therefore, healthier for the planet. Throughout America, small businesses, urban farming and hundreds of thousands of individuals participating in the Regreening of America can create a totally new fabric of life in cities.

Corporate-based services encourage the concentration and flow of money outside most urban areas. In contrast, mixed-use zoning, farmers markets and individually owned corner grocery stores are among many examples involving localized economic exchanges. A national organization known as Business Alliance for Local Living Economies (BALLE) supports and encourages the development of neighborhood-scaled commerce using these strategies.

The energy needed to produce and transport locally grown produce is significantly less than agribusiness-produced imports from California. Human accountability factors into strongly localized economies. Local producers often have direct contact with their end-use customers, so the incentive to produce higher quality is more immediate. In the world of localized thinking, economics is just one factor. Locally derived recycled water flows, energy flows, and mixed-use zoning in cities can all be associated with the BALLE concept.

Retrofitting and adaptive reuse: What about our existing building infrastructure? In most cities about 80 percent of the building stock that exists today will likely be occupied by successor generations of people. However progressive new construction sustainable design polices like the previously mentioned LEED program may be, the construction of new buildings will be far overshadowed by the urgent need to retrofit sustainable practice technologies into existing buildings, streets, and parking lots. This process is known as adaptive reuse. It is evident everywhere in older urban centers throughout America. The retrofitting of insulation, weather-stripping, and rainwater distribution system can be applied to most buildings. Opportunities for creation of community gardens and green spaces abound.

Making imaginative use of existing-building stock is an exciting venture. For instance, excellent examples of adaptive reuse can be found in Durham, No. Car. The downtown area of this city is dominated by brick warehouses and manufacturing facilities built by the tobacco industry over a century ago. Today these fine buildings have been adapted for condominiums and apartments which are in high demand.

Within the urbanized world we have the opportunity to transform how human populations will retrofit soft technologies into streets and buildings everywhere. We are envisioning an evolutionary green revolution leading us towards humankind's regained synergistic relationship with the natural world in cities. This transformative vision forms the heartbeat of the future ecorestorative green movement.

Social and Environmental Equity: Universal human participation is key to meaningful global ecological transformation. This not only bears repeating, it must apply to those who currently have little or no stake-hold in creating a sustainable society and urban environment in America's cities. Without the participation of millions of disenfranchised youth in urban America, the transformation of existing building stock is difficult to imagine. Celebrating the 75th anniversary of the Civilian Conservation Corps initiated during the 1930s, and akin to the Peace Corps launched in 1961, our political leadership has endorsed what is known as the Clean Energy Corps. The CEC's mission is to provide green collar jobs to hundreds of thousands of young Americans wanting to participate in the Re-Greening of America.

Billions of dollars are earmarked to fund an organizational structure and delivery systems creating the means for communities throughout America to provide a platform for Green Jobs Corps and Youth Build Programs.

Transforming buildings into nonextractive ecological contributors: Insofar as the built environment is concerned, we first begin with transforming buildings from extractive resource and energy components into benign ecological contributors. This idea is now being well received in the architectural design community. It means that it is now feasible, given a long enough period of time to render a return on capital investment, to build and retrofit buildings that produce at least as much energy as they consume. This concept has been popularized as "net zero" energy exchange between buildings and the electrical supply grid to which they are connected. In most cases, use of photovoltaic technology can achieve this objective in combination with a myriad number of devices designed more efficiently to deliver electrical power. A promising example creating more efficient use of electricity is LED lighting technology. This next generation of lighting fixtures is far superior to today's fluorescent technology. But as discussed before, application of "hard tech" solutions is not enough.

EcoRestorative Design: The application of ecorestorative design now comes into full focus. This is an approach to designing and retrofitting buildings in ways which complement use of both "hard" and "soft" technologies. Ecorestorative design sees buildings not only as energy harvesters; it sees buildings as one would see a coral reef in the ocean. In that way buildings can be seen as opportunities to enrich the fecundity of the Earth.

Why is this so important to us? The answer is that humanity can transform the way we use the land and the buildings upon the land so that the planet's bio-capacity is enhanced. As we have seen, at this very moment Earth's natural processes to produce life are slipping. Humanity must seek every opportunity to reverse this erosion of our life-support system. The time has come to envision buildings as biomass-enhancing ecological contributors to the planet.

Ecorestorative design makes use of buildings and their environs to help replenish Earth's ecosystems. Rendering both existing and new buildings into ecological contributors to the planet is very achievable. Doing so is a process of combining balanced rainwater flows with the nearby vegetative and microbial life that surrounds buildings. If we harvest rainwater and store it in ways that optimize building thermal-mass dynamics, and then use it to maintain controlled moisture levels in soil by means of irrigation, we can achieve the following:

-- increase microbiotic populations in soil through the interaction of buildings with surrounding landscaped areas (enhance fertility).

-- increase density of life populations per square meter of ground (enhance soil quality and therefore biomass production).

-- enhance biodiversity (through the application of permaculture and related Agrarian Earth Science principles).

-- lower the sine wave of building thermal variations (make it easier to maintain comfortable indoor air temperatures).

-- eliminate use of precious treated water resources for landscape irrigation applications (adopt the use of water conservation and on-site propagation and reuse patterns).

-- decrease rainwater flow velocity and volume over time (reduces storm water concentrations and runoff thus protecting riparian locales).

<u>The Transformative Urban Vision: Micro-Edens</u>: Micro-edens are places where nature is given a chance to reestablish herself on rooftops, vacant lots, streets, and anywhere open areas are exposed to sunlight. The majority of urban space is covered over with buildings, parking lots, streets and other impermeable surfaces. Innovative ways to transform

such life-compromising places are available thanks to the application of soft tech science. The application of permaculture tools, such as bio-intensive gardening, edible landscaping, and rainwater conservation techniques, can be retrofitted into cityscapes to make micro-edens.

We must visualize changing the extractive ecology of cities into exporters of energy and resources for food and planetary oxygenation. But most importantly, this vision sees masses of disenfranchised humanity with shovels in their hands. The application of Agrarian Earth Science is a labor intensive, site-specific process requiring large concentrations of participating people living in cities.

What underscores this blending of ancient and new technology? When we create green spaces, fertile ground, and havens for people, we at the same time are creating havens for nonhuman populations. When we step into this New Earth Story considering both the human agenda, and ~~as~~ care for the greater community of life, we find ourselves immersed in a story that is marked with compassionate, humane regard for nonhuman communities – “Our fellow astronauts,” as Dr. Buckminster Fuller would say.

The Heart of the Spirit of EcoRestorative Design Movement

These hard and soft technological ideas are important contributors toward addressing our environmental stewardship challenges. But they are not, in themselves, enough. There is a foundational prerequisite to the successful application of any technology and visionary idea. It is the underlying thing that shapes and guides how humans first perceive, and subsequently how they are then destined, to interact with the natural forces shaping their cities and neighborhood gardens. From this central point of attention is born the idea of ecospirituality. Thus begins the journey that saw the light of day in Hannover, Germany, well over a decade ago.

One can see how it is possible to commit ourselves to establishing ecorestorative beachheads in each city throughout the world. But the transformation of the human cityscape, to net ecological contributors to the planet, cannot hope for success without first sourcing from the depths of the human spirit a renewed sense of the sacred nature of all life.

What underpins, what inspires, what sets us upon a course of action with deep caring, spawns from what we are in our very depths. For our global venture to work out, the very soul of our Great Work, as Father Thomas Berry would put it, must be exposed to the light of day. The best of who we are is found in compassionate, humane regard for the firmament, and all that God has placed upon it. We are as the very ground we walk upon. We are in and of Earth – intimately connected to one another and all creation. Profoundly, ecorestorative thinking affirms the spiritual connection that exists between humans and the natural world.

In human endeavor, be it the arts, healing a child, or climbing Mount Everest, it is what we yearn to witness in ourselves and experience in life that drives and motivates us to climb any mountain, however daunting that mountain might seem.

It is for us, gathered here at Wesley Theological Seminary, and in faith communities throughout the world, to educate ourselves, and those who look up to us, about the sanctity of Earth and all its subjects. It is for us to educate our students, our neighbors, and one another in ways that will see us present to the profundity of life that surrounds every building, every garden, and every tree.

If those of us who are sharing the last heartbeats of this Symposium have a fresh perspective on what can be done, shall we then consider what we are to do? Shall we for a shared moment, reflect on the opportunity awaiting our impassioned commitment "to allow all future generations the right to life, and the right to participate in life processes equal in quality to that of our own time."

The Faith Community Challenge

I present you with a challenge. Let us consider having Wesley Theological Seminary, its outreach mission, and its sister faith communities, take on assignments which involve at least five aspects.

The first aspect is probably already clear to most of us–seeing the religious community actively committing to solutions and polices addressing environmental challenges of our time.

The second aspect of this challenge is to see Wesley Theological Seminary join with other higher education community colleges and universities in a commitment to adopt a carbon-neutral campus-wide plan. Such plans must be realized within the next two decades throughout America.

The third aspect appears already to be underway at Wesley Theological Seminary. The Seminary's campus, and its urban architecture, can be seen to be influencing policy through practical demonstrations. Through pursuing its own ecologically sound polices and projects, the Wesley Theological Seminary campus can contribute towards shifting faculty, student, administrative staff, and public awareness about sustainable alternatives. What lives at the heart of this challenge sees WTS, its affiliates, and local community members who see this campus as an educational demonstration resource, committed to environmentally sound practices. The WTS outreach vision can be committed to sharing the fruits of its sustainable and ecorestorative polices with the surrounding urban area here in Washington, D.C., and the faith community at large.

The fourth aspect may not be recognized by many people living in urbanized America. It is about rekindling our primordial connection with nature and the universe, as Father Thomas Berry would have us do. Out of the awe for the magnificence of Earth and its subjects, we can deeply enliven this Seminary's faculty, students, well-wishers, and participants to meet the environmental challenges that await us all. This is a rebirthing of what we may call an ecospiritual ecumenical movement. Such can be shared with clergy, laity, and the global community alike. Here is where human ecological nurturing finds its place in the ecorestorative process.

The fifth and perhaps most compelling aspect of this challenge is to take action. Before the conclusion of this Symposium, let us not leave this campus on Saturday without first determining a venue for the creation of a strategic task force. This task force would be mandated to pursue the four preceding ideas.

These ideas can only empower us if we come together in a decision-making body to deliberate, to discuss, to draw upon the group wisdom and its establishment of stakeholders at WTS, and every faith educational facility. The following offers ideas that can directly lead towards fresh commitment of resources and action plans.

Summary

In 1215 the "*Magna Carta Libertatum*" (the Great Charter of Freedom) required King John of England to proclaim certain rights (pertaining to freemen), respect certain legal procedures, and accept that his will could be bound by the law. In 2000, almost 800 years later, the international Earth Charter finds humanity expanding the notion of human rights by acknowledging the rights of all living communities on Earth.

Nature is becoming our most compelling great convener. This has set the stage for a new era of ecospiritual thinking which embraces the sanctity of all life on Earth. It is in this sense of the divine in all things that we can see awakening the human spirit in our time. A growing number of leaders within the faith community see environmental issues as moral issues addressing equitable consideration for all peoples, and for all life communities. Herein is the seed which all faith communities can water.

Today ever-increasing numbers of people around the world are feeling more concerned. Their attention is evidenced by international cooperative gatherings: Rio de Janeiro, Kyoto, as well as the Copenhagen Summit scheduled to convene during this Symposium. Such events hold promise that the human community is finally willing to come to terms with its failed environmental policies. In response to this growing evidence, we at this Symposium and Wesley Theological Seminary can take on a fresh leadership role in our communities. As community faith leaders, we have the ability to support growing international accord, as has been witnessed with the ongoing global "350" event.

We have considered traditional technological practice and integration of Agrarian Earth Science whereby the restoration of the planetary ecosystem can be undertaken by everyone, everywhere. We have looked at how buildings can be reconceived to restore the land areas surrounding them. We have seen how it is possible to rethink our existing building stock in ways that render the built environment net exporters of energy flows rather than the extractive nature of buildings today.

We have set forth a challenge that can be addressed by every faith and learning institution willing to educate everyone about sustainable alternatives. Most important to the purpose of this paper are the ideas and actions needed to meet these challenges.

I see our coming together as a gathering of impassioned individuals who are alive to their participation in the outcome of this great play now being co-scripted by both the human and non-human communities of earth. Out of this I have come to believe there is a new agenda before us. That agenda is our renewed and reverent dance with the natural world. From the eyes of every human being on Earth, nature herself is coming to dominate the human world agenda. Let us respond to that agenda in a humane, purposeful and dedicated way.

Our relationship and attitude toward the natural world significantly defines who we are. What lives within our hearts will shape our destiny with this planet. Above all else, our thoughts, attitudes, and perceptions about our innate relationship with the natural world are the keys to our future failure or success.

Bibliographic Resources

This partial listing provides further resources relevant to the topics presented.

www.350.org - focusing on the number 350 -- as in parts per million -- the level scientists know as the safe upper limit for CO^2 in our atmosphere. In December, 2009, world leaders will meet in Copenhagen to craft a new global treaty on cutting emissions.

www.aashe.org – Association for the Advancement of Sustainability in Higher Education (AASHE) – provides access to "Cool Campus!" a how-to guide for college and university climate action planning, and to their newly released Sustainability Tracking, Assessment, and Rating System (STARS).

www.climateprotect.org - Through its projects — Repower America, the WE Campaign, and the Reality Coalition — and its affiliated organization, The Climate Protection Action Fund, the Alliance seeks to present choices and offer changes that will protect our planet for future generations; http://greenerchoices.org/globalwarmingsavecarbon.cfm -- this website is an exceptional source of information for those who want to learn more about how they, as individuals and families, can reduce their "Carbon Footprint."

Spirit of the EcoRestorative Movement

www.livingeconomies.org – Business for Local Living Economies (BALLE) -- helping neighborhood businesses flourish in their local economies. And we're leveraging the power of local networks to build a web of economies that are community based, green, and fair local living economies.

www.engr.pitt.edu/mac/images-t/articles%20and%20docs/CleanEnergyCorps-Full%20Report-Web[1].pdf -- provides the full text document for the Obama administration plan to provide 600,000 green jobs to disenfranchised young adults affecting 15,000,000 buildings in urban America.

www.fore.research.yale.edu - The Forum on Religion and Ecology is the largest international multireligious project of its kind. With its conferences, publications, and website it is engaged in exploring religious worldviews, texts, and ethics in order to broaden understanding of the complex nature of current environmental concerns.

www.newmonkproject.org – a nonprofit nondenominational education resource for individuals and organizations dedicated to building the Earth from within, offering inspiration, support, and information on topics relating to eco-spirituality.

www.permaculture.org.au – originated the best known contemporary example of Agrarian Earth Science, known by many people as permaculture.

www.restoringeden.org – Christians for Environmental Stewardship – one among many sustainable policy advocacy student based organizations.

www.tlwarchitect.com – a resource of information on ecorestorative design and vision for the forthcoming "Regreening of America" and ecorestoration topics.

Further information on Micro-edens can be found in my article entitled "Rethinking Houses as Living Systems" in: The Ecozoic – Reflections on Life in an Ecological Age, a publication of the Center for Ecozoic Studies, Vol. One, 2008, Chapel Hill, NC.

Ecorestorative design makes use of buildings and their environs to help replenish Earth's ecosystems. Our underlying theme is to reeducate and redirect perceptions about western culture's relationship to Earth. To put this new thinking into action, we will entertain the opportunity to win America's enthusiastic support towards implementing a national green revolution – "ReGreening America." from "ECO-RESTORATIVE DESIGN" by Tim Watson

Our 21st Century Challenge: Redefining Sacred Space[1]

Rabbi Fred Scherlinder Dobb, Adat Shalom Congregation, Bethesda, Md.

By the logic of the burning bush, we should always be barefoot--for wherever we stand, we stand on holy ground. Today, kicking off a theme of this Symposium aptly titled "Transforming the Spirit," we look to the nexus of Spirit and space. Is there anywhere where God isn't?! Remember after Jacob's ladder, he awoke saying, "God was in this place, and I didn't know!" So it is everywhere, we believe–every spot is sacred. And just as each of God's children and God's creatures has a place in the plan, a reason for being there, and a justification for protection, so, too, does every place within Creation (at least every natural, sustainable, untrammeled place, a question we'll take up shortly). This is, to quote the session title that fell into my lap, "Our 21st Century Challenge: Redefining Sacred Space."

In these next few minutes, I hope to offer a series of useful[2] reflections on this question of sacred space, though daunted by the great wisdom

---

[1] Sizeable pieces of this talk draw on one which I gave on May 29, 2008, to the "Faith, Spirituality, and Environment" conference at Catawba College, Center for the Environment, Salisbury No. Car. My appreciation to Dr. John Wear, Juanita Teschler, and the other good folks doing great work in that special place.

[2] In terms of 'utility' I'm inspired by what I understand to be the legacy of Bishop and Dean Mathews -- who were and are challenging, as I hope these observations to be; who were and are effective organizers, as I hope some of these thoughts can be useful organizing tools or principles; and who connect/ed Spirit and society so seamlessly --

already in each of us gathered here. So really, I hope to set the stage for the sharing of useful perspectives, ideas, texts, approaches, resources – for that's why we're here.

So, best material first: God *IS* 'place.' Literally. A common Hebrew appellation for God is *Makom*, which translates as Place-with-a-capital-'P'. (It's best known in the greeting one gives mourners, *HaMakom yinachem etchem*, "May the place comfort you"). *Makom*/Place is both a given location *on* Earth, and a proper name for the Creator *of* Earth. This name of God, *Makom*, connects with a fairly recent subset of environmental thought, bioregionalism, whose adherents "are local caretakers. Dedicated to the concept of living-in-place, they espouse 'watershed consciousness' ... Bioregionalism advocates a new ecological politics of place." We become aware as creatures by developing 'a sense of place' (and developing that 'sense of place' is our bioregional mandate); we become aware as creations by developing a sense of God, *Makom*.[1] The more we know about our corner of Creation as a bioregion, as a place that supports life, the better we know the Creator. So our "21st century challenge" is not merely "redefining sacred space" – rather, the very notion of 'space' or 'place' itself rises to the theological plane. It is holy work, *avodat hakodesh*, to develop a 'sense of place.'

(Kudos, then, to the organizers of this very Symposium, for asking all attendees to bring a symbolic vial of water from a place special to them, for conjoined use in a closing ritual. This lets us celebrate the sacred

---

and anything that connects Spirit and society for us is useful. Sharing and convening, too, is another part of the Mathews legacy we invoke here.

[1] Carolyn Merchant, 217ff.; Fred Dobb, "The Rabbis and Expanding Environmental Consciousness," in Arthur Waskow's *Torah of the Earth*, Vol. 1, p. 163. Judith Plaskow also adds *makom* to her list of natural images for God, in *Standing Again at Sinai*, 165: "The traditional image of God as place (*makom*) evokes both the presence of the world in God and the extraordinary presence of God in particular places. As Rabbi Jose b. Halafta said, 'we do not know whether God is the place of His world, or the world is His place.'" (Plaskow seems to cite a different version of the quote that I know as the definitive Jewish statement on panentheism, from midrash Genesis Rabbah 68:9: *Hu m'komo shel olam, v'ein olamo mkomo* – "God is the world's place, but the world is not God's place.")

places in all our lives, and bring the best of 'our' places to whatever place we happen to find ourselves. We root the universal within the particular, and we bring our individuality to the conscious creation of community. Awesome.).[1]

So if we're tracking noteworthy approaches to sacred space, here's one: "**God is Place**." Indeed, loving a space is about loving the One who put that space in place, and vice versa. We may be familiar with theologian Martin Buber; *apropos* of our topic, Buber wrote:

> "...real relationship to God cannot be achieved on earth if real relationships to the world and to [sic] mankind are lacking. Both love of the Creator and love of that which [God] has created are finally one and the same. In order to achieve this unity, man must indeed accept creation from God's hands, not in order to possess it but lovingly to take part in the still uncompleted work of creation..."[2]

---

[1] Email to conference participants, early Dec. 2009: "**A Small Assignment for every Symposium participant:** Closing Ritual -- Bring with you a vial of water! / Do you live near a creek, river, pond, lake, brook or the ocean where you have watched that water rise and fall, freeze and melt, dry up and return again with the seasons? Is there a fountain in your community or at the town square of an office building? / The closing ritual at the Symposium on Saturday the 19th will involve water from our points of origin. Please take time to go out to the nearest source of water, or a place where the water is symbolic to you and recover some water (purity doesn't matter). Label the bottle with the source where you get it.... / Husband and wife / partners can bring water from a different source -- George, may bring water from Tampa Bay, and Carol from the pond behind their home. We would like water from as many different sources as we can possibly derive.... / Those who are flying, can get the 2 ounces on the plane... smuggle if you must. And, please, no fancy liquids – just the plain water of life...."

[2] Martin Buber, *On Judaism*, 209. Born in Austria in 1888, Buber revived Eastern European mystical 'Hasidism' and pioneered Jewish existentialism; barely escaping ahead of the Nazi killing machine, he became an Israeli peacenik; he died in Jerusalem in 1965. Buber's work has had greater influence outside the Jewish world than within, appearing in everything from Carter Heyward's Protestant lesbian theology, to Annie Dillard's spirituality-suffused nature observations. And *apropos* of Herman Greene's presentation, note Buber's commonalities with (and possible influence on) Thomas Berry, among other great contemporary ecotheologians.

Let that sink in: love of the Creator, and love of Creation, are finally one and the same. You can't have one without the other. The love of God we proclaim from the pews is *bubkis*, borscht, beans, if not backed up with concrete action in solidarity with Creation, with defense of that which our own hubris has imperiled. And in reverse, our 'secular' work on behalf of 'the environment' is made much more meaningful (and, well, 'sustainable') when approached reverentially, when seen as a slice of Ultimacy, of Godliness, of the Spirit. We take our humble place, over the long haul, not as users of Creation – and not just as creatures – but as co-partners in Creation's ongoing work.

Call that an amplification of "God as Place." But note the critical role of Relationship here – Buber after all was a theologian of relationship, best known for his 1923 classic, *I and Thou*. Religious leaders who routinely exhort relationship with the One must be equally passionate in facilitating relationship with Creation, without which we have no relationship with God. And as befits all things ecological, what we have is a much less hierarchical set of relationships than we often think. Not humanity *over* nature or *versus* nature, but *with* nature, as part of nature. (Phyllis Trible wrote that in Genesis 1, the human "is both apart and a part" – apart from, and a part of, the rest of Creation – though DNA research pegs us as much more mammal than angelic being, forcing a reappraisal of Psalms 8 and 19 and other sources!). Thus Buber's echo of traditional Jewish thought, that "we are copartners with God in the ongoing work of Creation." So, second, "**build a deep, enduring, largely egalitarian *relationship* with Place**."

Place, or places? What is an ecosystem but a large set of adjacent individual places, and isn't nature the set of all ecosystems? Can we treat any one place in isolation? [Meant as a rhetorical question, this became a focal-point of discussion: no we can't, in theory; yes we must, in practice; "no, yes, and then again perhaps;" see the adage "think globally, act locally;" etc]. Places are interconnected, as are we – and, significantly, as are our faiths. A truth appropriate for a conference devoted to founders of the Ecumenical Institute: we must look beyond our own tradition/s, to respond to today's challenges.

Noting how environmental problems "cross boundaries of religion and culture" as well as political borders, ecophilosopher J. Baird Callicott in his article "Multicultural Environmental Ethics" [1] uses the migratory routes of an endangered bird, the Siberian crane, to illustrate. These routes "extend from shamanic Siberia through Eastern Orthodox Russia, cross Buddhist Tibet, Confucian China, and Islamic Afghanistan, and end in Hindu India." Callicott summarizes three ways in which these many thought systems can come together to protect a natural inheritance common to all their lands. First, in the ecological approach, "each cultural-national entity retain[s] its autonomous authority to make conservation policy within its jurisdiction, in the hope that over time a unity, balance, and harmony among them will emerge naturally;" of course, such a balance may never come, at least not in time to save the Siberian crane. In the very problematic second "hegemonic" approach, one culture simply "dominates all others." Foreign to Reconstructionist Judaism or the United Methodist Church, this is a model still too much in vogue elsewhere, including among extreme elements within each of our faith traditions. Callicott's ideal third way, an "orchestral approach," takes its inspiration from "the unity-in-multiplicity that is the human condition at the advent of the third millennium;" here each cultural-national entity is like an instrument in an orchestra, playing notes which harmonize or overlap with one another without sacrificing each instrument's unique tone.[2]

Though we chose to participate in this symposium's Environmental Stewardship track, here we must also be the "Interfaith Engagement" track – and Urban Mission, and Corporate Social Responsibility – and Health, and Education. Though "ecologically relevant texts do not necessarily result in ecologically appropriate actions,"[3] religion does give us a sense of values–many held commonly, within and across faiths which can meaningfully ground our efforts to defend Creation. Here, urgency

---

[1] J. Baird Callicott, "Multicultural Environmental Ethics," in Tucker and Grim, *Daedalus*, p. 78.

[2] Callicott, pp. 79, 82, and 84.

[3] Mary Evelyn Tucker, *Worldly Wonder*, p. 24.

helps. Says Rabbi Ismar Schorsch: "In many cases it's extremely difficult for different religions to cooperate, and a bit of pressure from the outside is very salutary. I think that's exactly what the ecological crisis offers."[1] As Huston Smith muses, "Twenty-five hundred years ago it took an exceptional man like Diogenes to exclaim, 'I am not an Athenian or a Greek but a citizen of the world.' Today we must all be struggling to make these words our own."[2] How true, in light of today's dire environmental realities. So, three-'a', **we must develop a sense of Place**. And three-'b', **the interconnections at the heart of ecology serve as an interfaith lesson**, too.

So how to balance micro and macro, "place" and "places"? The Holy Qur'an and the ancient Midrash both say that "saving one life is like saving the world," since each of us is like a hologram, a manifestation of the whole. Does that work for space? Well, yes and no. The alpine forest is not the intertidal zone is not the oak savannah is not the peat bog. With few exceptions (like the red-winged blackbird, the only avian found in every single county of all 50 states!), what thrives in one place, one ecosystem, will not fare well (or at all) in another. Places are not interchangeable. "Home is where the heart is," but "sweet home Alabama" is not "my old Kentucky home" is not "my New York state of mind"[3] – your house growing up wasn't hers, or mine -- "O Canada my home and native land" is not the Fatherland, or Mother Russia, or the "*artzeinu* / our land" of Israel's anthem "*Hatikvah*." (The latter may in fact be, or overlap greatly with, the "our land" of Palestine. Contested places, and possibilities for coexistence therein, is a whole can of worms which is not unrelated, though I'm not going there today![4]).

---

[1] Ismar Schorsch, in Rockefeller-Elder, *Spirit and Nature*, p. 185.

[2] Huston Smith, *The World's Religions*, p. 7.

[3] As Rev. Margaret Helen Aiseayew said in our group's introductions, "the participant biography says I'm 'a Midwestern farm girl,' but that's not quite so – I'm an *Iowa* farm girl!"

[4] See Marlin Jeschke's ***Rethinking Holy Land: A Study in Salvation Geography*** (Scottsdale PA : Herald Press, 2005).

So places are unique, just like people. And just as no one person knows everything (certain special Jewish prayers are said only with a *minyan* of ten, a quorum through which we transcend ourselves, and challenge our own assumptions and norms), so does not every place enjoy ultimate wisdom, or self-sufficiency. We need to fight like hell to protect *this* place, our place -- but also to protect that one, and that one, and those too.

What's true for people and for places is true for species as well -- the inherent value of biodiversity is in a sense identical to that of multiculturalism. (We're all in this together; "all God's critters got a place in the choir," as do all people, as do all faiths). Recall that human beings alone, near sunset on the world's first-ever sixth day, merit no comment; unlike the mammals which preceded us by a matter of hours or even minutes, we are not even called *tov*/"good." But the interconnected whole of which we are a part – an ecosystem, a biosphere, Creation in its relational interdependent fullness – that is *fabulous*: "*Vayar Elohim et kol asher asah*, And God saw all that God had made; and 'yo!,' *v'hineh*! – it was *tov me'od*, very good" (Genesis 1:31). Four, then: "**Places are unique, interconnected, and interdependent; save the one, *and* save the all**."

Five: can the spaces we build, even atop and in the stead of what God once placed there, be holy and worth of protection, too? Yes. Sorta. The built environment is just that, environment (and built!). Little boxes made of ticky-tacky rarely win aesthetically or spiritually over the wetlands and forest they replaced, but folk gotta sleep somewhere (the doubling in one generation of per-capita cubic footage to heat and cool and furnish, though, is troubling). And what of the Spirit or holiness that's evident in local landmarks – think the National Archives, the Library of Congress' magisterial Jefferson building, Maya Lin's Vietnam Memorial (and some might re-add "the White House" this year!). Are these not worth celebrating, exploring, defending? People and their built places should not be regarded as blots on the landscape; but we have to work hard to not become scars on it, either. There's nothing holy about a West Virginia mountain whose top thousand feet are dynamited off for its seam of coal to fuel our rapaciousness; there's but debatable holiness in a row of box stores surrounded by countless acres of sterile impermeable treeless parking lots. Still, the key point here is that "people count" – and this is a key contribution of religion to environmentalism, the idea that we're created in God's image (*b'tzelem Elohim*) and thus each possess infinite value and worth, and with it, the idea of "environmental justice." So five, "**people build great places too, sometimes**." Which brings us to:

Six-The corollary: "when we build, we should only build well." As my friend (documentary filmmaker) Judith Helfand says, "don't just build a building; build a *just* building." For no type of building is that more true than for a house of worship. How ironic to clear-cut forests for the beams and joists dedicated "to the glory of God;" to come together on Sabbath to a structure that just leaks its energy; to pay our day laborers below-living-wage salaries as they prepare the site and raise the walls where we'll sing *"Halleluyah, Allah-hu-Akbar, Om-Shanti."*

I'm happy to report that our Bethesda, Md., synagogue, Adat Shalom Reconstructionist Congregation, did design a low-impact building that received the EPA Energy Star Congregations award, and did lobby its subcontractors to ensure that no one who helped build it (and today, no one who cleans it) would make less than a living, not a minimum, wage. And I'm happier still to report that Adat Shalom and all of us have been leapfrogged (and the bar set incredibly high) by our sister synagogue in Evanston, Ill., Jewish Reconstructionist Congregation, the first-ever house of worship anywhere to receive the rare LEED-Platinum certification for their stunning, sacred, sustainable synagogue building. I now commend JRC's fabulous virtual tour and online description to one and all – www.jrc-evanston.org/green_synagogue[1] – we all have much to learn from it.

---

[1] Accessed 1/28/09. It is one-stop shopping for congregations seeking ideas on building green. From the planning phase, an excellent concise overview by Rabbi Brant Rosen is up at http://www.jrf.org/omer07-BRosen. A full green description of Adat Shalom and JRC is found in chapter eight of my D.Min. thesis, written for Wesley Theological Seminary (under Dr. Bruce Birch and others involved as well in this Symposium), accessible at http://scherlinders.wordpress.com/2009/05/08/freds-thesis/.

And this is all 'sustainability': not just passive solar-sitting and zoned-HVAC systems, recycled or natural flooring and as much FSC-certified 'sustainable' wood as we can find, reused or local materials, low-wattage lighting and appliances, and other elements of ecological sustainability--but ethical, social, and spiritual sustainability as well. Helpful resources are available through the wonderful Interfaith Power and Light[1] movement, and elsewhere. Again, "...don't just build a building, build a *just* building." A just, sustainable, embodying-the-spirit building.[2] More, later in this Symposium's environment track, from Tim and others, on the power of architecture to serve all the highest, and only the highest, purposes. So yes, six: "**build sustainably, or don't build**".

That's a fine half-dozen thought-provokers on space and sacredness, I hope. Let's make it ten (with no detail or sidebars this time!), then open this up for the important work of introductions and collaborations,

---

[1] www.interfaithpowerandlight.org – full disclosure, I write as chair of the steering committee of Greater Washington Interfaith Power and Light (www.gwipl.org). And in a lovely connection with this Symposium, GW-IPL would not exist but for key support from two vital organizations – the Churches' Center on Theology and Public Policy, and the InterFaith Conference of Metropolitan Washington – both founded under Bishop James K. Mathews!

[2] On this, think LEED, and think Interfaith Power & Light. An *excursis*: Rabbi Abraham Joshua Heschel (author of the magisterial "The Prophets" and "The Sabbath" among other key works) famously said, "neutrality is not an option." That prophetic stance is more applicable now than ever, given the need for "80 percent reductions by 2050." When it comes to the collective need for carbon neutrality, one's individual neutrality is simply NOT an option. In other words, we need commitments like LEED for our intermittent huge projects of new construction or retrofitting; these simply must be pursued whenever our institutions go into capital mode. Our Interfaith Power & Light model, on the other hand, is applicable for all congregations and all folks, anytime – we engage congregations and clergy and parishioners from the entry-level of "swap a lightbulb here, give a green sermon there," all the way on up to "pursue LEED." We see a real multiplier effect when we educate our faith communities to help our *communal* religious buildings make green choices, at which point hundreds thousands of congregants and visitors (who are also consumers, businesspeople, decision-makers and citizens) are touched by that vision, and hopefully are moved to carry it forward. Our work is not only sacred, but it is potentially huge. Let *that* sustain us!

expansions and rebuttals and clarifications, and ultimately progress together, for which we're here. So, quickly --

Seven: **Time and Space both count, with Sabbath connecting them** – the Sabbath, which Abraham Joshua Heschel called "a palace in time" – or in reverse, a sacred time whose practices help us sanctify space in turn. To stay sustainable over the long haul, we need *Shabbos*, as it's pronounced in the Ashkenazi/Yiddish tradition. Jewish unionists a century ago, facing oppressive working conditions, said on Fridays, "*sha*, shut up, *boss*"! – you're not the owner of me; there is a realm more important than economics, than bringing home the bacon (!), than dollars and cents and profits and earnings. *Shabbat* the realm not of doing, but of being, said Heschel. Our deliverance requires our rest. Jurgen Moltmann saw this clearly: "The day of 'the new creation' presupposes the ecological 'day of rest' of the original creation, if that new creation is to complete the first and not to destroy it. The ecological day of rest should be a day without pollution of the environment – a day when we leave our cars at home, so that nature too can celebrate its *Sabbath*."[1] *Shabbat*, in time, helps us save space through a lowered impact, and a healthier sense of priorities. An Orthodox Rabbi in 19th century Germany, at the very dawn of industrialization, saw this clearly; Samson Raphael Hirsch first channeled the prevailing voice of his (and our) era, then responded in his own: "'Sabbath in our time?! To cease for a whole day from all business, from all work, in the frenzied hurry-scurry of our age! To close the exchanges, the workshops and the factories, to stop all railway services – great heavens! The pulse of life would stop beating and the world perish!' The world perish? On the contrary, it would be saved."[2] Our souls need

---

[1] Moltmann, 296. His section on the Sabbath opens (277) with an ode which deserves to appear alongside Hirsch's and Heschel's here: "In the Sabbath stillness men and women no longer intervene in the environment through their labour. They let it be entirely God's creation. They recognize that as God's property, creation is inviolable; and they sanctify the day through their joy in existence as God's creatures within the fellowship of creation." His hope (139) in people "discovering the meaning of their lives in joy in existence, instead of in doing and achieving" – and reflection that "Without the Sabbath quiet, history becomes the self-destruction of humanity" – are just as eloquent.

[2] Samson Raphael Hirsch, *Judaism Eternal*, 2:30 – circa 1850's. See also Heschel, that most poetic German-then-American Rabbi-philosopher who escaped the Nazis,

Shabbat. Our bodies need *Shabbat*. Our world – Creation – needs *Shabbat*. We need it, in order to make sustainability itself sustainable. (Ironically I'll have to miss ecoworkshops three and four, since those fall on our Jewish Sabbath!).

Eight: Law – and the idea that **Spaces must be preserved by law**. What might Jewish environmentalism contribute to the larger faith-community and secular ecology world? There are lots of partial answers, but only two which are truly unique. *Shabbat* as a day (and Sabbatical and Jubilee as cycles of) detachment from the ever-faster merry-go-round of modern life, which we just addressed; and law and regulation, as a good thing. Paul famously and unfavorably compared the 'old' Judaism as a religion of law, with his new Christianity as a religion of love. He was partly wrong: Judaism has plenty of love, and Christianity has its fair share of law as well. But inasmuch as he was right, I want to celebrate Judaism's legality, its insistence on focusing on day-to-day choices and conduct, on setting rules and clear do's and don'ts (since should's and shouldn'ts clearly don't suffice; where did the last eight years of "voluntary efforts" to curb carbon emissions leave us?—Warmer). Think Copenhagen;[1] think cap-and-trade or carbon-tax or whatever works; think regulation, and law, to protect the places (as well as the people and the critters) we love.

Nine: **place and proximity -- care about near, and also about far**. It's no accident that Leviticus (19:18) formulates the golden rule as *v'ahavta l're'akha kamokha*, "love your neighbor as yourself" – neighbors being the ones in your space, or near it. We do naturally, and must, start with

---

marched arm-in-arm with King in Selma (saying later of it that "my feet were praying), and like his good Reverend-Doctor friend risked institutional wrath by early decrying the war in Vietnam – Heschel said it like this: "To set apart one day a week for freedom ... a day on which we stop worshipping the idols of technical civilization, a day on which we use no money, a day of armistice in the economic struggle with our [fellows] and the forces of nature – is there any institution that holds out a greater hope for [our] progress than the Sabbath?" (The Sabbath, 1951, p. 28).

[1] We gathered on the final day of the global summit on climate change in Copenhagen; hours after this presentation came the announcement that an accord had been reached, though it fell far short of what many of us hoped for in terms of concrete emissions reductions targets and a firm near-future date for a final, binding agreement.

those closest to us. But we can't end there, either, especially in today's "global village," when all people are "neighbors." Further, we must consider non-human neighbors in Creation, as well. Rabbi Hillel (in the double-digits BCE) expressed this tension well – "If I am not for myself [or we are not for ourselves], who will be for me? But if I am only for myself [if we are only for ourselves], what [not who, what, he ups the ante here] am I? And if not now, when?"

And ten: to state the obvious – "**with the gift/miracle of Place, comes Responsibility**." We learn this in perhaps the top "Jewish environmental text" (for pith and quotability and impact), found in an ancient midrash on Ecclesiastes (Qohelet Rabbah 7:13). It speaks of the primal place, Eden, and it speaks too to today's ecological concerns, especially to climate change's "fierce urgency of now" (and yes, that is an intentional MLK reference; today's climate movement needs precisely an injection of the commitment we know from the civil rights movement,[1] since all humans and all of Creation are indeed "caught in an inescapable network of mutuality," as King wrote from that Birmingham jail):

בשעה שברא הקדוש ברוך הוא את האדם הראשון, נטלו והחזירו על כל אילני גן עדן ואמר לו

ראה מעשי כמה נאים ומשובחין הן וכל מה שבראתי בשבילך בראתי. תן דעתך שלא תקלקל ותחריב

את עולמי, שאם קלקלת אין מי שיתקן אחריך.

When the Holy Blessed One created the first human, God toured this human around all the trees of the Garden of Eden, and said to the person: "See My works, how beautiful and praiseworthy they are? And everything I have created, I have created for you. Be mindful -- that you

[1] As my GW-IPL colleague Mike Tidwell just wrote in the Washington post (12/6/09) exhorting strong collective and political action on climate change, beyond the popular focus on small individual actions: "The country's last real moral and social revolution was set in motion by the civil rights movement. And in the 1960s, civil rights activists didn't ask bigoted Southern governors and sheriffs to consider "10 Ways to Go Integrated" at their convenience."

do not curse [ruin] and devastate my world -- for if you ruin it, there will be no one after you to repair it.[1]

And finally, from Rabbi Tarfon from the early second century CE, collected among the aphorisms of the tractate of the Mishnah called *Pirkei Avot* (which translates variously as "ethics or chapters of the ancestors / founders") – a reminder that as we go on protecting places and redefining sacred space, we must not be done in by the scope of the challenges, not buckle under the weight of the world, not give up when you see others not playing their part,[2] but rather we must "keep on a-walkin', keep on a-talkin,' marching to the freedom land." Tarfon said:

> It is not upon you to complete the task – but neither are you free to avoid it.[3]

"It is not upon <u>us</u> to complete the task – but neither are <u>we</u> free to avoid it.

Thank you.

---

[1] Kohelet Rabbah 7:13; original translation after that of Avram Reisner et al, in *Hekhsher Tzedek al Pi Din* 18.

[2] In a 2002 ethnography-in-the-congregation interview with me, Carol from Adat Shalom admitted, "it's so huge: [people seem to feel] 'you're not going to get *everyone* to do it, so why should *I* bother'?!" This text, now a popular song as well ("*Lo Alecha*"), should be the antidote.

[3] Mishnah Avot 2:16, original translation.

ReThinking the Purpose of the Church and Its Ministry

E. Maynard Moore, Ph.D., Vice President, WesleyNexus.org

It has now been more than sixty years since the appearance of the Niebuhr-Williams-Gustafson study of theological education in the United States and Canada. This was a formative and comprehensive analysis led by Professor H. Richard Niebuhr of the Yale Divinity School, initiated by the Board of the American Association of Theological Schools, and supported by a charitable foundation grant from the Carnegie Corporation of New York. But despite this study's wide and quick acceptance, and the range of subsequent books on the subject, few structural changes in theological education appeared in this country. The confusion of purpose among mainline Protestant churches, the lack of a clear conception of what is required in theological education, and the educational mediocrity that these authors discovered continued to prevail in most of our seminaries.

Of course, Niebuhr had been writing on this theme for some years previously. Niebuhr was also the theological mentor of Joseph Wesley Mathews, for whom Joe Mathews had produced more than 500 pages of a dissertation that would have earned him a doctorate if he had chosen to submit it through the accepted channels. And it is clear that Niebuhr continued to have a strong influence on Joe Mathews in subsequent decades. As one combs through Joe's collected papers, one finds scores of Niebuhr's articles and papers underlined and digested, with ideas and notations that show up in numerous papers and lectures which Joe developed subsequently.

Niebuhr authored the book The Purpose of the Church and Its Ministry as the first volume to emerge from this extensive study, which appeared in 1956, and which was on the required reading list when I began my own seminary education a few years later. I don't remember any instance or occasion when the book or its recommendations were implemented in the seminaries or in the churches we were serving at the time. When one reads the book today, one gets an immediate sense of relevance coming from the principles on which the author and his collaborators, Daniel Day Williams and James M. Gustafson, drew their insights and conclusions.

One can discover dozens of passages in Niebuhr's book that could easily appear in one of Joe's lectures. Here is one:

> "What is the function of the minister in the modern community? The answer is that it is undefined. There is no agreement among denominational authorities, local officials, seminaries, professors, prominent laymen, ministers or educators as to what it is or should be. This lack of agreement is a characteristic feature of the situation today, and accounts in a large measure for the low educational status of the ministry." (Niebuhr, p. 51).

Here is another:

> "Denominationalism not the denominations; ecclesiasticism not the churches; Biblicism not the Bible; Christism not Christ; these represent the chief present perversions and confusions in Church and theology today. There are many other less deceptive, cruder substitutions of the proximate for the ultimate. But the ones identified seem to set the great problems to faith and theology for our time. In them the need for a constant process of a radically monotheistic reformation comes to appearance." (Niebuhr, p. 46).

Niebuhr and his associates tried to provide some clarity on the rightful purpose of theological education by defining the theological school as the "intellectual center of the church's life" where the faith of the church seeks understanding. They spoke of a "double function" for the seminary: on the one hand, "It is that place or occasion where the Church exercises its intellectual love of God and neighbor;" and on the other, "It is the community that serves the Church's other activities by bringing reflection and criticism to bear on worship, preaching, teaching and the care of souls." (Niebuhr, p. 110).

Understood broadly, this definition and double function affirms the traditional concept of theological education in terms of a more or less co-equal emphasis on the so-called "theoretical" and "practical" disciplines. However, even if such an emphasis can be constructed and maintained, the question remains as to the adequacy of such a scheme for the demands of our time. As Dean Gerald C. Brauer of the University of Chicago Divinity School once pointed out (1967, p. 335) "Nothing better guarantees the inability of seminaries to fashion a genuine professional degree than the built-in split between the so-called practical and theoretical fields."

One can imagine that Joe Mathews felt this tension deep in his gut, and it may have been one of the factors that contributed to his decision to leave seminary teaching just about the time that Niebuhr was writing. The inadequacy of the prevailing conception of educational methodology lies in its taking for granted inherited relationships between seminaries and churches and in passing over some important questions that have to do with the place and purpose of the church in contemporary society. That might be one of the driving forces behind the rest of Joe Mathews' life and ministry, first in Austin and later in Chicago.

The general result was that, instead of a creative interaction, the relationship between the seminary and the churches was more often an unhappy marriage, ill-conceived and unsupported, debilitating to the theological enterprise and something less than fulfilling for the churches. Niebuhr and his associates at least raised the question of the "purpose of the church" and discussed theological education within this context, but they did not deal adequately with functional relationships between the two. Several other studies in the field did not even raise the prior question, but Joe Mathews did. For him, the imperative was clear: there must be a radical rethinking and subsequent redefinition of the entire relationship between theology and the churches.

The Quandary of the Churches

Sixty years later, churches still hear the call for "renewal" from every quarter, but a built-in institutional hesitancy and lethargy seem to compromise all genuine attempts at reform even where there is some vision of the future. The number of "experimental ministries" is burgeoning, but these remain isolated, short-lived and restricted in scope and purpose. There is virtually no long-range denominational and ecumenical planning beyond the sphere of the general church extension enterprise and few have any hope for a creative breakthrough in life and mission from this quarter. This general shortsightedness is one price we pay for a too-narrow institutionalism, and the unwillingness to risk resources in a comprehensive approach to common problems is slowly dragging the church deeper and deeper into a quagmire of irrelevance.

Of course, there are people of vision in the church, but as yet these folks have not been heard with the sense of urgency necessary to transform the vision into reality (see Rose, 1966) With few exceptions, people of vision are isolated from levers of power, and the church as a whole is yet too comfortable within its cocoon to open anything but a back door to institutional change. The church, however, will not be able to challenge the twenty-first century to a new humanism, unless and until old patterns of mission are discarded, allowing the Gospel to "come alive" in new and more appropriate forms.

How might we recover and ground a theological vision that will move us from the mainline back to the "frontline"? I cannot speak for any of the institutional churches in the mainline, not even for those in my own heritage of United Methodism. But I can recover some basic tenets out of that tradition, back to John Wesley--who thought a lot about these questions--and I can rethink some of the questions that Niebuhr and his associates were asking about the purpose of the church and its ministry. In doing so, I believe I can demonstrate that others can do it from within their own ecclesial traditions, even in a way that we might learn from each other and forge some collaborative initiatives in the future.

I matriculated to Perkins School of Theology just a few years after Joe Mathews left for the Christian Faith and Life Community in Austin, which is where I subsequently took RS-1 and spent a number of weekends in seminars. While at Perkins I studied Patristic Theology with Dr. Albert C. Outler, and forty years later I have come to a deeper appreciation of the grounding this provides for my theology as well as for my understanding of Wesley and the United Methodist Church. In the paragraphs to follow, I will make reference to the continuum of developing Patristic pneumatology, and connect it to the "Wesleyan Spirit" as taught by Dr. Outler, and conclude with a few implications for our "ecclesiology" for the 21st century.

Rediscovering the Apostolic Church

If Wesley was indeed "a quite conscious primitivist" in his ecclesiology, as Outler contends, might this have implications for those of us who would consider ourselves to be "modernists" or even "post-modernists" (in the meaning of John B. Cobb, Jr., 2002, see esp. pp. 1-33). It would at least seem to be consistent with the leadership of Bishop John R. Schol in the Baltimore-Washington Conference, who has launched a well-defined program called "the Discipleship Adventure" that aims to see 600 Acts 2 churches flourishing in the Conference by the year 2012 (see www.bwcumc.org for details). Let's agree with Dr. Outler's assessment that for Wesley, "Both the apostolic church and the church of the early fathers were vivid models for him in his program of Revival." (Outler, 1991, p. 75). What does this mean for us in the Protestant mainline today?

Conceding that this question deserves a full and complete paper of its own accord, if not an entire monograph, allow me to comment on just three areas of importance, and reference Wesley's own statements as a point of departure. I believe these remarks can be considered consistently with some of the things I learned from Joe Mathews as well. These I will identify as (a) the church as a means of grace, (b) the church as a community of saints, and (c) the church as the presence of the Spirit.

First, **the church as a means of grace**. And perhaps we must establish some meaning of the term "grace," not just for Wesley's understanding but in terms which mean something to the (post-)modern mind. For me the best place to ground this notion is Paul's sermon to the Athenian intellectuals in Acts 17, where he proclaims that "God is not far from each one of us. For 'in Him we live and move and have our being'." (v 27-28). At the outset we concede that Paul is quoting Greek philosophical poetry, specifically Epimenides the Cretan who wrote an ode in praise of Zeus:

> They fashioned a tomb for thee, O Holy and high one,
> The Cretans, always liars, evil beasts, idle bellies!
> But thou art not dead; thou livest and abidest forever,
> For in thee we live and move and have our being."
> (cited in Bruce, 1980, p. 359).

Such ideas were not uncommon among the Stoic writers, so Paul's listeners were on familiar ground. But Paul, of course, was not identifying the Christian God with Zeus but affirming that the sustaining divine presence truly "is not far from each one of us." In fact, what Paul says is that God has created humanity in the world in order that "they would search for God and perhaps grope for him and find him" – though indeed, "he is not far from each one of us" (v. 27). We can readily see the affirmation that we live in our diverse locations and time periods ("limited by our boundaries and habitations"), but in seeking, we sometimes do find God -- <u>because God is, in fact, so near to each one of us</u>.

Now what is so interesting to me is John Wesley's commentary on this passage, found in his <u>New Testament Notes</u> on Acts 17:27ff. Wesley offers his approval of Paul's sermon, describing the triadic line from Epimenides as "one of the purest and finest pieces of natural religion in the whole world of pagan antiquity." Michael Lodahl (pp. 117 ff) thinks that Wesley's observation here about "natural religion" applies equally as well to Wesley's use of the phrase "natural conscience" when he speaks in other places of the dynamic interaction of God with human beings at every place and every time in their actual concrete socio-cultural circumstances. This is nothing less than God's prevenient grace understood in terms of the sustaining nearness of God to all human beings in their "situatedness" (a Joe Mathews word), their concretely historical environs. To make the point more firmly, Wesley continues in his comment on verse 28: "We need not go far to seek or find [God]. He is very near to us; in us. It is only perverse reason which thinks [God] is afar off." Indeed, this is the God whom Martin Buber characterized as "closer to me than my own I." (Buber, p. 79).

Of course, Wesley's pronounced emphasis on God's immediate, life-empowering presence must be understood within the social and historical context of his resistance to 18th century Enlightenment deism, for Wesley would brook no notion of a deistic God, nor of an autonomous, self-sufficient human being. His doctrine of God was much too rich in its appreciation of the classical categories of divine omniscience and omnipresence. And his anthropology was too rooted in the Greek Church Fathers' vision of human "participation" in the divine life to resort to the notion of the autonomous "enlightened" individual. For Wesley, we are embodied souls, material creatures living in a "God-drenched" world, called to live toward God, even as we now live in God. The implication is that we cannot -- however much we try -- live outside of God's sustaining presence: to be outside of God's creative and ever re-creating, life-bestowing and nurturing Spirit is to die, "to return to our dust" (Psalm 104:29). Wesley concludes his comment on verse 28: "This denotes [God's] necessary, intimate, and most efficacious presence. No words can better express the continual and necessary dependence of all created beings, in their existence and their operations." (Wesley, NT Notes, on Acts 17:28).

The implication for the Church becomes very evident. God's grace is the Good News that is our mandate to proclaim, just as did Paul to the Athenians. For Paul, Jesus as Christ was to be seen as the fulcrum point through which all history is transformed, and so the church is assigned the task of continuing this mission of transforming the world. The church, as a means of God's grace, proclaims and fulfills God's message of judgment and mercy. More specifically, the church fulfills the mission through its solidarity with the "others" of history, just as did Jesus in his ministry to the poor, the downtrodden, the oppressed, the marginalized of our society. According to Luke, the kingdom is presented to the "others" of history when they receive the power to speak and to determine their lives for themselves (see Green, 1995). The church exists among those who have received God's message of love and freedom, and fulfills its mission when it proclaims this message as Gospel. As Dean

Rebecca S. Chopp puts it, "Luke challenges and invites us to begin where the church is--in ministry and mission of Jesus among the marginalized of the earth, and from this place to work towards the transformation of history itself." (Chopp, in Meeks, 1995, p. 98)

The Community of Saints

Second, let us turn to **the church as a community of saints**. Outler contended that Wesley felt free to interpret Article XIX "more comprehensively than its authors ever intended" (Sermons, 1991, 3:45). The historic language reads:

> "The visible Church of Christ is a congregation of faithful men, in which the pure Word of God is preached, and the sacraments be duly administered according to Christ's ordinance, in all those things that of necessity are requisite to the same."

As Collins points out (2007, pp. 238 ff), this definition of the Church, especially as employed during the Reformation, not only made allowance for the rise of the great national churches (including the Church of England), but it functioned as a standard to distinguish doctrinal error from corrupting practices. And as a consequence, Wesley's catholic sensibilities were so strong that he could not exclude from the church catholic any congregation in which unscriptural doctrines are sometimes preached, nor those where the sacraments were being provided without sanction. In short, Wesley would always be generous in speaking of those members of the body of Christ who, though they may be mistaken in some of their beliefs, were nevertheless motivated by love, charity and works of mercy. To make this point, Wesley would hearken back to the language of the Apostle's Creed to affirm the reality of "the holy catholic church," (as e.g. Sermons 3:55-56):

> "The church is called holy because Christ the head of it is holy.... Nay, the shortest and the plainest reason that can be given, and the only true one, is: the church is called holy because it is holy; because every member thereof is holy, though in different degrees, as he that called them is holy."

To support his claim, Wesley would quote St. Paul in I Corinthians,

> "To them that are sanctified in Christ Jesus," referring to those who are part of the *ecclesia* who have been called out of the world, who are thus sanctified, and are therefore saints.

Wesley loved the festival of All-Saints' Day (See Journal, November 1, 1767), and often utilized the Collect for All-Saints' Day from the 1662 Book of Common Prayer, revering God "who hast knit together thine elect in one communion and fellowship." The Gospel lesson for All-Saints' Day is Matthew 5:1-12, in the Beatitudes where Jesus promises to the pure in heart the vision of God, the substantive theme affirming the communion of saints. Wainwright concludes from this: "The Collect stresses we are in the body of Christ. Then the Epistle suggests that this is a fellowship of praise to God's glory. The Gospel reveals the nature of sanctification and sainthood. And on this path to perfection and the final kingdom of divine glory and our joy, we have the example of the blessed saints" (Wainwright, 1995, p. 238).

Further, Wesley liked to reference the New Testament church as described in Acts 5:10, as "called by the Gospel, grafted into Christ by baptism, animated by love, united by all kinds of fellowship, and disciplined by the death of Ananias and Sapphira." (NT Notes, 287). As Collins observes, Wesley could thereby promote the Methodist movement to be in conversation with the broader catholic church for the purpose of reform, while inclusively defining the church as already a peculiar people called holy because Christ is holy, and as such, the church is always called to live in a way that befits the saints (Collins, 2007, p. 240). Outler characterized this dialectical tension as a "blend of Anglican and Anabaptist ecclesiologies." ("Introduction," Sermons, 3:46).

For us moderns, the implications would seem to be two-fold. On the one hand, we have few grounds for attempting sanctions of exclusion on the basis of doctrinal disputes. Although doctrine and "right belief" was important for Wesley, this was not sufficient reason to withhold the hand of fellowship. Not even "faith" itself was determining for Wesley. As Wesley said in his 1746 letter to a Mr. John Smith:

> "I would just add, that I regard even faith itself, not as an end, but as a means only. The end of the commandment is love, of every command, of the whole Christian dispensation. Let this love be attained by whatever means, and I am content; I desire no more. All is well if we love the Lord our God with all our heart and our neighbor as ourselves."
>
> (Wesley, Works, Vol. 12:78-79, Letter to Mr. John Smith, June 25, 1746.)

And on the other hand, working from within the ranks of the faithful, the task is never complete, we must always work to make real the characteristics of "holiness," to do all that we can to provide support, instruction, and opportunity for those among the baptized to live lives that embrace the principles of love, charity and hope in the world. One cannot comprehend John Wesley's ethics without grasping this point: moral living is absolutely necessary to a life of holiness. As Rebekah Miles remarks: "For Wesley, it is not just a fruit or an evidence of a holy life: it is a means of grace necessary to nourish the holy life" (Miles, 2002, p. 98). In Collins words,

> "For if the church is no longer aiming at the inculcation of holy love, as the point of it all in the lives of its members, if it fails to demonstrate the universality of such love by being deflected with parochial concerns, then in Wesley's judgment, it has lost its way no matter what institutional or objective elements remain in place." (Collins, 2007, p. 240)

The Church as People of Spirit

Thirdly, let us consider **the church as the presence of the Spirit**. We find a lot in Wesley's writings explicating the presence of the Holy Spirit in the church, usually in the context of his observations about Christian "assurance." This becomes clear in three of his Sermons: "The Witness of the Spirit, I" "The Witness of the Spirit, II," and "The Witness of Our Own Spirit." Without trying to preach these sermons all over again, let us simply make a few comments to show Wesley's main point.

Here it is impossible to speak about the mission of the church being fulfilled if it is not demonstrated by "the fruits of the Spirit" (for interesting psychological comments of the "fruits of the Spirit," see William James, 1961, pp. 194 ff). In a word, we are to live out the truth of Romans 8:16, which speaks of the spirit "bearing witness *with our spirit* that we are children of God." As Wesley put it in his second sermon on the Spirit, "To secure us from all delusion, God gives us two witnesses that we are his children. And this they testify conjointly. Therefore, 'what God has joined together, let not man put asunder.'" What this means is that while the "witness of the Spirit" itself may be ineffable, an incommunicable experience, nevertheless, if it is genuinely present, then "love, joy, peace, patience, kindness, generosity, faithfulness, gentleness, and self-control" (Gal 5:22), will also be present.

While this does not mean that the church can ever "look inside" a person's heart to confirm "the witness of the Spirit," still, the Christian community is uniquely privileged to judge whether or not the Christian believer is living in such a way that the "fruits of the Spirit" are manifest. As Clapper points out (2002, p. 116), it is a common misunderstanding concerning "sanctification" to identify the fruit with certain "experiences" or inner feelings of holiness. But, in fact, when one considers the terms "sanctification" and "experience," one realizes that these are "relational" terms. One cannot love without loving a particular someone, one cannot have joy without being joyful about something, one cannot have inner peace except in relationship to potential sources of experience. And, Clapper concludes, "This is true for all nine fruits of the Spirit, and John Wesley knew that to grow these fruit, one had to be in relationship with both God and one's fellow human beings. That perhaps is the clearest implication of Wesley's often-quoted statement that there is no such thing as holiness without social holiness."

For Wesley, love of God and neighbor, the so-called "holy tempers," are founded on works of mercy, and are always organically and intrinsically related. He made this very clear in his Sermon "On Zeal:"

> "In a Christian believer, love sits upon the throne, which is erected in the inmost soul; namely, love of God and man, which fills the whole heart, and reigns without a rival. In a circle near the throne

> are all *holy tempers*: long-suffering, gentleness, meekness, goodness, fidelity, temperance – and if any other, [it] is comprised in the "mind which was in Christ Jesus." In an exterior circle are all the works of mercy, whether to the souls or the bodies of men. By these we exercise all holy tempers: by these we continually improve them, so that all these are real *means of grace*."
>
> (Works, 3:385. sec 1).

We must always be clear that Wesley guards against any claim that such fruits, such "works of mercy" imply that we thereby earn our salvation. Nothing we say or believe or do can thus merit God's pardon. Rather, such works are a means of grace for a life of holiness. In his sermon "On Visiting the Sick" (Works: 3:385-86, Sec 2), Wesley writes, "The walking herein is essentially necessary, as to the continuance of that faith whereby we are already 'saved by grace,' so to the attainment of everlasting salvation." As Rebekah Miles concludes (in Chilcote, 2002, p. 101),

> "These works are not optional then, but necessary for the Christian life. On the one hand, when Christians practice works of mercy in love, their love increases, their holy tempers (patience, gentleness, etc.) are exercised and improved, and they grow in grace. On the other hand, when they fail to practice them, they 'do not receive the grace which otherwise they might. Yea, and they lose, by a continued neglect, the grace which they at first received.'"

As with the Christian, so with the church. Wesley never made this more clear than in his admonitions on charity and stewardship. Works of mercy are expressions of our love for God and for our neighbor and a channel for the means of grace by which the church fulfills its mission by caring for the least and the lost. For Wesley, nothing would be more clear on the Day of Judgment. In his sermon "On the Danger of Riches" Wesley exclaims:

> "O ye Methodists, hear the word of the Lord! I have a message from God to all men, but to you above all others... Weep and howl for the miseries which shall come upon you. Your gold and your

> silver is cankered, and the rust of them shall witness against you, and shall eat your flesh, as if it were fire. Certainly it will, unless ye both save all you can and give all you can.... By the grace of God, begin today!" (Works, 3:240, Sec II, 9)

In this circular process, failure-to-give promotes a further callousness of the soul towards the poor, which hinders later works of mercy, and is quite simply an actual antithetical act towards the works of mercy as a means of grace. And when the failure marks the fellowship of the church as a whole, we abandon Christ's mission in the world–which for Wesley (as for St. Paul) was to abandon Christ himself. It was a struggle that occupied Wesley his entire life, and toward the end, he was convinced he had failed. He might be just as despondent were he able to observe Methodism in America at the beginning of the 21st century.

Once this nation's largest Protestant denomination, and still a leader in the so-called mainline of American Protestantism, United Methodists have become "respectable" in all aspects of religion and community life. Many consider this a hallmark of the "success" of Methodism. But in our move up the socio-economic ladder, as we embrace the "center," we leave behind those at the margins. From this perspective, voices from the margins – if they are heard at all – are ignored as irrelevant or are branded as "special interests." But what if, as Joerg Rieger asks (2003, pp. 15 ff),

> "What if not the center but the margins were able to grasp what really matters? Can the margins once again, as in the days of the early Methodist movement, point us to a new future? This question has implications far beyond the Methodist movement itself."

Wesley himself seemed to have a premonition about this "mainstreaming" of Christianity. Dr. Outler's oft-repeated claim that Wesley promoted a "high-church evangelicalism" has been used by many in our pulpits to argue that we can have it both ways. But, as history shows us in a myriad of examples, such a stance seldom works. The logic of the center usually requires alignment with the powers-that-be, and a gospel based solely on popular morality is fundamentally flawed. In

Wesley's unmistakable words, "If you are walking as the generality of men walk, you are walking into the bottomless pit." (Sermon 31, "Sermon on the Mount, XI," Sec III.4, Works, 1:672.)

There is some recognition of this in our midst. In 1996 the United Methodist bishops issued a challenge to our church through the acclaimed Children and Poverty: An Episcopal Initiative, reminding us that "what is at stake is nothing less than the reshaping of the United Methodist Church in response to the God who is among the least of these." (cited in Heitzenrater, p.7). But we in United Methodism shortly discovered that we really have no institutional way of changing the basic structure of socio-economic relationships working from the center. In the spring of 2001, the United Methodist bishops reaffirmed their earlier challenge:

> "We are convinced that the reshaping of the church and the proclamation of the Gospel cannot take place apart from a newly developed sense of community: that is, the relationship of the church (including the bishops) with the economically impoverished and the most vulnerable of God's children. God has chosen the poor, the vulnerable, and the powerless as a means of grace and transformation."
>
> (http://www.umc.org/initiative/statement.html)

The bishops backed up their challenge with a full-fledged theological argument that includes references to Jesus' own way of relating to people on the margins of our society, relating this to the core of our Methodist traditions, suggesting that a new understanding of the church as a means of grace might be the first step. Means of grace are channels through which we receive grace into our lives as faithful Christians, and for us, we have to recover what Wesley meant when he expanded the traditional Anglican works of piety (prayer, Bible study and Holy Communion) with the works of mercy.

As Rieger points out (2003, p. 25), this changes the conventional wisdom completely:

> "As channels of God's grace, works of mercy not only have an impact on those who receive them but also on those who do

> them. We can no longer talk about works of mercy as "outreach" activities from the haves to the have-nots. Works of mercy become tools of what for lack of a better word might be called "in-reach," tools for the reformation of the church itself."

John Wesley understood this. He saw this in Jesus' ministry at every turn, and found it substantiated in the writings of the early Church Fathers, those "radicals" in the first three centuries to whom he pointed his preachers as models for discipleship in his own time. Dr. Outler once wrote (Outler, 1964, "Introduction," p. 10):

> "It was the ancient and Eastern Fathers' tradition of *disciplined* love that became fused in Wesley's mind with his own Anglican tradition of holiness as *aspiring* love, and thereafter was developed in what he considered to the end as his own most distinctive doctrinal contribution."

For Wesley, the essence of the matter is "the love of God, controlling every part." (see Vincent, 2003, p. 38), and the challenge from Mr. Wesley today is "practical divinity," or love *in praxis*, the radical obedience of the totally committed life. This would be manifest as the "movement of the Spirit" where God joins in the suffering of those who exist (barely) on the margins of our society. (see Rieger, 2001, p. 174.)

In the Wesleyan tradition, the aim of theology must be understood as the "reform of the nation, most especially the church." ("The Large Minutes," Q 3, Works, Sec 299). As Ted Jennings reminds us, "Without the continual impetus to be reformed, the church becomes nothing more than the religious form for a world that is passing away, rather than a concrete and dramatic sign of the coming reign of God." (Jennings, in Rieger and Vincent, 2003. p. 53).

Conclusion

So, I conclude. I have tried to show that Wesley's theology was, at its core, pneumatological, and that his theology was grounded both in Scripture and the Patristic Tradition that comes to us out of Chalcedonian thinking, particularly from the works of the Eastern Church Fathers. To the extent that this is sound, I owe this understanding to Dr. Albert

Outler, for whom both the Fathers and Wesley were pillars of sound theology for the people called Methodists. I take solace in thinking that it is due to the soundness of this theology that both Joe Mathews and his brother Bishop James K. Mathews found their own calling and defined their own ministries within this tradition, and helped spread this message to "people of spirit" around the world.

Of course, we live in a much wider world than did either the Patristic Fathers, John Wesley or the Mathews brothers, so today we have to theologize in a much more broad context. Today, listening to the voices from places still considered by many the margins of Christian theology -- such as the voices of women, and liberationists, and green theologians -- sensitizes us to the necessary pluralism of *pneumatological* thinking. Attention to the voices of the Third World provides enrichment to classical theology, not only because the rapid expansion of the Christian church is taking place outside the West, but also because the vivid spiritual life of these voices is a greenhouse of new insights into old doctrines. I have no doubt John Wesley would be fully engaged in this enterprise of "practical divinity" in our time, and I genuinely believe that H. Richard Niebuhr would have his heart gladdened by observing such a movement reborn, but I wonder if Joseph Wesley Mathews would have the patience for doing theology in today's broader context? I don't think he would hesitate – he would "just do it."

Sources Referenced

Brauer, Gerald C. 1967. In "Discussion: The Seminary in Ten Years," *Union Seminary Quarterly Review,* Vol. XXII, No.4, May 1967.

Bruce, F.F. 1980. Commentary on the Book of Acts Grand Rapids, Eerdmans Publishing Co.

Buber, Martin. 1956. I and Thou (2nd edition). New York, Charles Scribner's Sons.

Chilcote, Paul W. (ed.) 2002. Wesleyan Tradition: A Paradigm for Renewal. Nashville: Abingdon Press.

Chopp, Rebecca S. "Anointed to Preach: Speaking of Sin in the Midst of Grace, " in Meeks, M. Douglas (ed.) 1995. The Portion of the Poor. Abingdon: Kingswood Books.

Clapper, Gregory S. 2002. "Making Disciples in Community," in Chilcote, Paul W. (ed.) 2002. Wesleyan Tradition: A Paradigm for Renewal. Nashville: Abingdon Press.

Cobb, Jr., John B. 2002. Postmodernism and Public Policy: Reframing Religion, Culture, Education, Sexuality, Class, Race, Politics and the Economy. Albany: State University of New York Press.

Collins, Kenneth J. 1997. The Scripture Way of Salvation: The Heart of John Wesley's Theology. Nashville, Abingdon Press.

Collins, Kenneth J. 2007. The Theology of John Wesley: Holy Love and the Shape of Grace. Nashville, Abingdon Press.

Green, Joel B. 1995. The Theology of the Gospel of Luke. New Testament Theology 3. Cambridge: Cambridge University Press.

Heitzenrater, Richard P. 2002. The Poor and the People Called Methodists. Nashville: Abingdon Press, Kingswood Books.

James, William. 1961. The Varieties of Religious Experience: A Study in Human Nature, with an Introduction by Reinhold Niebuhr. (originally published 1901). Macmillan Publishing Company.

Jennings, Theodore W. "Breaking Down the Walls of Division: Challenges Facing the People Called Methodist," in Rieger and Vincent (2003), pp. 53-65.

Lodahl, Michael. 2003. God of Nature and of Grace: Reading the World in a Wesleyan Way. Nashville: Abingdon, Kingswood Books.

Maddox, Randy L. 1998. Rethinking Wesley's Theology for Contemporary Methodism. Nashville, Abingdon Press, Kingswood Books.

Meeks, M. Douglas (ed.) 1995. The Portion of the Poor: Good News to the Poor in the Wesleyan Tradition. Nashville, Abingdon Press, Kingswood Books.

Miles, Rebekah. 2002. "Works of Mercy as Spiritual Formation," in Chilcote, Paul W. (ed.) 2002. Wesleyan Tradition: A Paradigm for Renewal. Nashville: Abingdon Press.

Moltmann, Jurgen. 1969. Religion, Revolution and the Future (New York: Charles Scribner's Sons).

Moltmann, Jurgen. 1977. The Church in the Power of the Spirit, (tr. by Margaret Kohl) (New York: Harper & Row Publishers).

Niebuhr, H. Richard. 1956. The Purpose of the Church and Its Ministry: Reflections of the Aims of Theological Education. New York: Harper & Brothers Publishers.

Outler, Albert C. (ed.) 1964. John Wesley (New York: Oxford University Press).

Outler, Albert C. 1991. The Wesleyan Theological Heritage: The Essays of Albert C. Outler. ed. Thomas C. Oden and Leicester R. Longden. Zondervan Publishing House.

Outler, Albert C, and Richard P. Heitzenrater. 1991. John Wesley's Sermons: An Anthology. Nashville, Abingdon Press.

Rieger, Joerg. 2001. God and the Excluded: Visions and Blind Spots in Contemporary Theology. Minneapolis: Fortress Press.

Rieger, Joerg. "What Do Margins and Center Have to do with Each Other?' Chapter 1 in Rieger and John J. Vincent. 2003. Methodist and Radical: Rejuvenating a Tradition. Nashville: Abingdon, Kingswood Books.

Rose, Stephen C. 1966. The Grass Roots Church. New York: Holt, Rinehart and Winston.

Sugden, Edward H.(ed) 1983. John Wesley's Fifty-Three Sermons. Nashville, Abingdon.

Swete, Henry Barclay. 1912. The Holy Spirit in the Ancient Church: A Study of Christian Teaching in the Age of the Fathers. London: Macmillan & Co, Limited.

Vincent, John, "Basics of Radical Methodism: Challenges for Today," Chapter 2 in Rieger and Vincent (2003).

Wainwright, Geoffrey. 1995. Methodists in Dialogue. Nashville: Abingdon, Kingswood Books.

Weber, Theodore. 2001. Politics and the Order of Salvation: Transforming Wesleyan Political Ethics. Nashville, Abingdon Press, Kingswood Books.

Wesley, John. 1909. The Journal of John Wesley (ed. by Nehemiah Curnock) (New York: Eaton & Mains). 8 volumes.

Wesley, John. 1931. The Letters of John Wesley (ed. by John Telford) 8 volumes (London: Epworth Press).

Wesley, John. 1952. Explanatory Notes Upon the New Testament (London: Epworth Press; reprinted 1960).

Wesley, John. 1958. The Works of John Wesley 14 volumes (Grand Rapids: Zondervan Publishing House

Theological Education in the 21st Century: A Global Vision

Bruce C. Birch, Ph.D., Dean Emeritus, Wesley Theological Seminary

I never met Joe Mathews. I came as a student to Perkins School of Theology after he had left for Austin. But I was deeply affected by his work and his legacy. He left a mark on the school of theology at SMU, and I heard many stories and testimonies to his passion and commitment for raising up the leaders the church would need for the future. That, after all, is what theological education is all about. Some of the raising up and equipping of leaders happens in theological schools, and some of it happens elsewhere. Such equipping of leaders for a new church in a new world happened everywhere Joe Mathews located himself, and wherever his network of church renewers stretched.

That network touched my life at Iowa Wesleyan College in Mt. Pleasant, Iowa, where I came as a new faculty member in 1968 at the same time as did the new campus chaplain, Morris Bratton. Morris had been with Joe Mathews in Austin, Texas, and I think largely because of his presence there, a number of the college age children of the community in Chicago at the Ecumenical Institute became students at Iowa Wesleyan. Those students included John Mathews who was in one of the first classes I ever taught.

At Iowa Wesleyan I took my first RS-1 and CS-1 courses, and eventually many more. I was soon teaching RS-1's, many of them. That curriculum is deeply implanted and has continuously influenced my theological thinking. I believe I read everything in the "suitcase library." The movement for the renewal of the church that Joe Mathews spawned deeply shaped my vision of the church I wanted to be a part of.

But there were two Mathews brothers, and my path has crossed with Bishop James K. Mathews as well. To my delight, he was appointed as the resident Bishop of the Washington Area where I have now been an elder in full connection for thirty-eight years. For 8 of those years James K. Mathews was my bishop, and we had many interactions because he became very deeply involved with Wesley seminary, as a member of its Board of Governors, as a founder of the Churches Center for Theology and Public Policy, as an adjunct faculty member and mentor to many students, and as a continuous friend and conversation partner with seminary administration and faculty to this very day. I have been privileged to be a theological educator with Bishop Jim as a colleague.

These two brothers, Joe and Jim, are two of the shaping visionary figures of my church universe, and it is my good fortune that their vision was large enough to encompass not only the church, but the world.

My assigned task in this session is to talk about Theological Education in the 21st Century. It is a fortunate time to have such an assignment because winds of change are blowing in theological education, and they are, I believe, the winds of the Spirit. A new vision is emerging in theological education, and the preparation of leaders for the church in the 21st century is already looking quite different than the seminary education I knew at Perkins in the early 1960s. If he could see it now, Joe Mathews would be both amazed and gratified. Brother James is still a part of these changes, and he is, I believe, both proud and hopeful.

I will have to speak personally about these things. I have been a faculty member at Wesley Theological Seminary for thirty-eight years until my retirement from full time responsibilities this past July, and the last eleven of those years was in service as the Dean of the seminary. I think what I have seen happening over that time at Wesley is representative of what is happening across theological education. So I will use Wesley as a positive case study because in spite of the challenges, I think Wesley has largely embraced those changes. Wesley's current strategic plan, adopted in 2004, is entitled "Ministry 2044" because forty is the biblical number for a generation, and Wesley is committed to educating for the next generation of church leaders, not for the one just past.

Out of my experience and vantage point at Wesley I want to lift up some convictions about the characteristics of emerging theological education that will serve the challenges of the 21st century, and I will concretize those characteristics out of my own experience.

1. Theological education for the 21st century must be in the context of the diversity of the whole body of Christ.

When I joined the faculty of Wesley Theological Seminary in the fall of 1971 there were no full time ethnic faculty members and only one woman. We were a group of white males, and I was the youngest by a gap of 11 years. The student body wasn't much different. There were three women in the M. Div. program and only 5 percent of the student body were African American or Asian and no Hispanics. The average age was lower because it was before the big wave of second career students arrived in the 1980s.

Today's reality is very different. The faculty is about 50 percent each male and female. There are seven African American faculty, two Asian, but unfortunately no Hispanics. The student body is 59 percent women and 41 percent men in the master's degree programs. The student body is 56 percent white and 44 percent non-White ethnic with African Americans as the largest group at 119 students. There are 59 Asian students but only 9 Hispanic students. There are 29 International students. I have no statistics from the days when I began in 1971 for denominational or theological diversity, but at present 55% of Wesley students are United Methodist with the remaining 44 percent spread over 35 different denominational traditions. When people have asked me what it is like to teach at Wesley I have often said it is like teaching in a cross section of the body of Christ.

I am using Wesley as a case study but I am aware that this profile is not typical everywhere. Some denominational traditions are less open to those of other religious traditions and mainly educate only those of their own tradition (e.g., Roman Catholic and Lutheran). But I think Wesley represents the direction of seminary education for the 21st century. The patterns by which persons attend and join congregations is less and less dominated by denominational loyalty. My wife pastors a sizable United

Methodist congregation and new member groups come from a wide variety of backgrounds with only a few lifelong Methodists. This diversity is reflected in Bible study and small discussion groups. They are eager to know the marks and distinctive traditions of their congregation and it's Methodist background, but they value and are shaped by the traditions that shaped them in earlier life. Pastors in the 21st century need to be prepared for a rich ecumenical mix even inside of particular congregations.

This, of course, is fully consistent with Joseph and James Mathews' understanding that church renewal must be an ecumenical enterprise. The future of the church can honor and be enriched by particular denominational traditions but they cannot live in denominational silos.

Theological education for the 21st century has to self-consciously embrace the varieties of the human family as the only context worthy of the gospel, and pastors must be educated to open their congregations to this diverse human family in creative ways even when immediate surrounding demographics make this a challenge.

To the diversities I have named must be added those of economic class. In particular no responsible theological seminary in this century can fail to sensitize its graduates and the church's future leaders to the scandal of poverty in a world with the resources to feed everyone. Poverty in our neighborhoods and around the world is a failure of will and not of resources, and church leaders must be equipped to address this reality and mobilize the compassion and justice of congregations. To fail to do so will make the church increasingly irrelevant because linked to poverty are a host of other challenging issues that threaten the future of our world. These include racism, nationalism, environmental degradation, adequate health care, adequate education.

The diversity of the church is also its most important resource in providing an adequate biblical, theological, spiritual and liturgical base for linking love of God and the well-being of our neighbor. We are enriched by a growing diversity of worship styles, preaching idiom, theological contexts and perspectives, and patterns of spiritual formation that grow out of our human diversity and helps direct our response to the challenges of the 21st century world. We worship, study and pray better when we are enriched by the wide variety of persons and cultures encompassed by the body of Christ.

2. Theological education in the 21st century must be global in its vision and in its commitments.

One could hardly imagine two church leaders with a more global vision than the Mathews brothers, Joe and Jim. They understood in all their leadership efforts that the vision for the church of the future must be global, and the breadth of places around the world represented in this gathering is a witness to their global efforts. The renewal sought by Joe Mathews in the Ecumenical Institute could not be confined to efforts in Chicago's Fifth City or even to the churches of the U.S. The Institute for Cultural Affairs embraced global vision and global reach. The global vision of James Mathews took him to India where the church would not leave him because they needed Episcopal leaders to urge the church to a truly global consciousness adequate for the 21st century, and he has been tireless in raising global consciousness and creating global networks both for the United Methodist church and as a tireless ambassador to the global ecumenical church.

No conception of theological education to prepare leaders for the 21st century could keep faith with the Mathews brothers' legacy if the perspective of that education was not global in scope. But in institutional terms this is easier to say than to do. It requires some fundamental alterations in consciousness and commitment of resources.

When I began seminary teaching 38 years ago theological education had some faculty of vision who sought out of their own experience to bring the world into the classroom, but the fundamental enterprise of theological education was fairly local and regional in its orientation. There were some international students whose presence helped create some consciousness of the church beyond the boundaries of North America, and some of these students have gone on to become great leaders in the world church. Some faculty led travel-study programs to various parts of the world, but these were expressions of individual faculty interest and not of institutional commitment.

But particularly in the 1980s there began to be a concern for and a discussion of what was called "the globalization of theological education." The American Association of Theological Schools became committed to the importance of this enterprise and sponsored conferences, consultations and publications in this area. Some foundations became interested in this concept. Perhaps the most important of these was an effort by the Plowshares Institute under the leadership of Robert and Alice Evans and with the support of other foundation funds that launched a project in the globalization of theological education that took the entire faculties and key administrators from a representative group of almost twenty theological schools on global immersion trips to meet leaders in the global church and experience their ministries. These schools were then challenged to develop a project in their own schools that concretely sought to embody a greater global vision in the enterprise of educating church leaders.

Wesley Theological Seminary was one of those schools, and I think those trips were transformational to the school. In small groups with faculty from other schools, the Wesley faculty traveled to China, Peru, the Philippines, South Africa, Mexico, El Salvador, and other regions that escape my memory. We were also challenged to immerse ourselves in the other worlds of our own cultural context. So the entire Wesley faculty traveled to the southernmost county in West Virginia for five days and spent four nights in a hospice in inner city Washington, meeting with leaders and experiencing the ministries in those places.

The local project that resulted from this experience was the institution of a cross-cultural requirement of all students for the M.Div. and the M.A. degrees, and a commitment of the Wesley faculty to continuing participation in the leadership of this program. Every student must spend two to three weeks immersed in experiencing the ministries of the church in a cultural context different from their own. There was tremendous resistance to this in the beginning. Some argued that students couldn't afford it, that students often had jobs or churches that would not allow them such time away, that faculty would consider this an extra load to their present teaching, that the school would have to add personnel to administer such a program. But after several years the voices of dissent around this program disappeared. The experiences of students and faculty alike were transformational and they gave witness to fellow students and faculty on the value of this. It continues to be a central part of the Wesley program. Wesley was one of a handful of schools to adopt such a requirement in the 1980s but it is becoming much more common in theological education today.

From such stirrings at Wesley came the adoption in 2004 of the school's current strategic plan, which includes as one of the five major goals for the school: *to become a truly global seminary*. The intermediate steps cannot be chronicled here, but the important thing to note is that from an additional degree requirement Wesley now understands global vision and commitment to be fundamental and foundational to the whole enterprise of theological education.

From my perspective as Dean at Wesley for the past eleven years here is what I would describe as the most fundamental change. Wesley has moved from programs that merely enrich the perspectives of its own students (a worthy goal) to engaging in genuine partnerships that help strengthen the preparation of leaders around the world. Enriching our own students is not enough. We have to participate out of an abundance of resources compared to much of the world in building the world church.

This is consistent with the vision of the Mathews brothers who were never content to bring wider vision to the immediate locales where they lived and led. They were constantly fostering enterprises, entering partnerships, channeling resources, sending people, bringing people to further the sense of the church as an interconnected global enterprise that we are all a part of.

For theological education one of the greatest challenges of the 21st century is how to prepare and equip leaders fast enough for the growth that is taking place in the church in Asia, Africa and Latin America. Wesley has felt that one of our most important missions is to partner with efforts to educate leaders around the world. Educating leaders for the church is our business; how can we assist partners in the world church to develop educational programs and institutions that will serve their long-term needs?

Wesley now has a Vice-President for Global Initiatives, Dr. Kyunglim Shin Lee, and she is tirelessly traveling the globe in brokering these partnerships. Our goal is not to have global extension campuses of Wesley like some large universities can do. Our goal is to support, assist, provide scarce resources (often faculty) for ongoing enterprises of theological education in places struggling to establish themselves and meet the challenge of providing needed leadership.

Wesley has been involved in three joint Doctor of Ministry programs with the seminaries of Europe in providing leaders with advanced training to themselves lead programs that are extending to reach growing churches in Eastern Europe and the territories of the former Soviet Union. Nine Wesley faculty have directly taught in the seminary in Moscow helping bridge the gap while indigenous leaders complete the doctoral work to fully staff their own programs.

We are beginning our fourth Doctor of Ministry program in partnership with the Methodist Theological University in Seoul, South Korea. These programs are giving advanced preparation to leaders in the Korean churches and missions worldwide but also extending to educate promising leaders in Southeast Asia many of whom already have responsibility for building theological education programs in their own country.

Wesley has supported and sent faculty to teach in a pioneering program in the Yucatan that has produced the first ordained Mayan pastors in the Mexico Annual Conference of the United Methodist Church.

We have an ongoing relationship with Africa University in Zimbabwe, where Bishop James Mathews served as Episcopal leader for a time. This includes bringing promising students every year to Wesley for a semester of study as well as sending faculty who have taught in the Zimbabwe program and receiving faculty who have taught for Wesley.

In February of 2010 two Wesley faculty members will be teaching in the seminary in Liberia and consulting on how Wesley might partner to strengthen that program.

These are just a few examples for one seminary. Other seminaries are likewise extending themselves in partnership to strengthen theological education around the world but unfortunately these are still a decided minority. In fact, in the context of the current economic crisis some schools have responded by becoming more insular and self-protective. This is a tragic miscalculation. There is no chance that we will not increasingly need to think and act globally, in our lives, in our churches, and in our ministries. Too many theological schools are still educating leaders to serve in a church that will not meet the needs of persons living in the 21st century.

3. Theological education in the 21st century must be unreservedly committed to the church but open in respect to the reality of an interfaith world.

In many ways this assertion is an extension of the previous discussion on the globalization of theological education, but it deserves separate treatment. Since not all of the world is Christian, increased global awareness and contact will bring us into interfaith contexts. But even domestically the U. S. has a large and growing population of adherents to other religious traditions. Theological education has a very poor track record of preparing pastors to understand and meet this interfaith world. In the context of global tensions this is even more imperative.

Bishop James K. Mathews has, for many years, been one of the most important voices in urging the church to give attention to interfaith conversations, a commitment nourished undoubtedly by his experience in the interfaith climate of India but by no means limited to that context. Joseph Mathews intentionally shaped the global outreach of his own movement in terms of the meeting of cultures and not in terms of the extension of the church or the Christian faith.

I wish I could be more encouraging at the direction of theological education in these matters, but I think many schools still regard interfaith understanding and conversation as an "enriching extra" but not of central importance. I believe that Wesley has made a significant start in this area. Most importantly we added Dr. Sathianathan Clarke to our faculty as professor of theology, culture, and mission and now holder of the Bishop Sundo Kim chair in World Christianity. Coming out of the Church of South India, his is one of the most important voices helping the church relate to an interfaith world, and his presence is transforming the Wesley community. We have added courses in interfaith theological perspectives and in particular religious traditions to the curriculum, and the faculty has added a course requirement in this area to the requirements for the M.Div. degree. We have Muslim and Jewish faculty teaching adjunct courses at Wesley including a current visiting faculty member from Turkey. Some of our cross-cultural immersion options for students now include interfaith dimensions and experiences.

Even these things are just a beginning--and many schools have not even made this beginning. The need for a leadership equipped to understand and relate to an interfaith world will only grow as the 21st century progresses. The Mathews brothers would only encourage us to redouble our efforts.

4. Theological education in the 21st century must be committed to explore new forms of pedagogy, new structures of curriculum, new technologies, and new ways of envisioning the church.

Theological schools are not only places for learning and research by insightful faculty. They have to be places of effective teaching and innovative centers for visioning and learning. Both Joseph and James Mathews were teachers, whatever else they were. They boldly and effectively cast the age-old gospel message into new and effective forms. The RS and the CS curriculum was a rich and innovative addition to the educational landscape of the church. The design of an RS-1 using papers, art works, films, innovative course design and theory was ahead of its time.

Now, for some, the jury may still be out on charting as an educational technique, but it was a pedagogical tool that engaged many in serious theological conversation–persons who had no previous skill or practice in the world of theological ideas. But now they were charting Tillich! Bishop Mathews became my Bishop here in Washington, and I know that the first year was not out before he had the entire clergy membership of the conference engaged in producing an educational resource that was then shared and used by the laity in the entire annual conference. He was a teaching bishop *par excellence*. He was the only person I ever knew who could use the invitation to give the benediction for a teaching moment.

The theological school adequate to the 21st century will have to be a place that recognizes the huge changes taking place in the way people learn, the methods and technologies now available, and the way these things are changing not only our culture but the church. Worship services are now routinely incorporating media components into the worship experience. Students come to seminaries with previous university experience in online education, use of course software to enhance the classroom experience, and curricula that incorporate opportunities for a variety of learning styles.

Seminaries are behind the universities in these areas but many are making strides in closing the gap. It is important to note that these have developed at such a rapid pace that not all new pedagogies or learning technologies are used with equal quality of educational experience. We cannot begin to innovate for the sake of innovation. We cannot embrace new practices without claiming them to serve our core vision and mission.

I was in the large room under the chapel in 1988 when the faculty all opened the boxes of our first office computers and received beginning instruction in the MS-DOS operating system. None of them even had color screens. Now classrooms routinely have computer and media equipment that could not even have been dreamed of at the start of my teaching career. The growth of the Henry Luce III Center for the Arts and Religion at Wesley has created an awareness of resources for learning beyond the printed page. Efforts have been made to help faculty develop pedagogies that are effective and practical in the use of these capabilities.

Nontraditional ways of structuring curriculum and schedule are now commonplace. Wesley offers courses in the daytime and the evening, in Saturday classes and intensive January terms. We are now offering a number of online courses in areas we believe are adapted to this method of learning. We have unique videoed resources in United Methodist history, doctrine and evangelism with over 50 scholars worldwide giving lectures filmed at Christ Church, Oxford. Our faculty have been sent to pedagogy workshops sponsored by the Wabash Center, a preeminent center for educational method in theological education, and we received an invitation to participate in a three-year project called the Lexington Seminar to improve faculty teaching.

This is all important because the church and world into which religious leaders are sent is changing in these same ways. The Mathews brothers urged us by their own example to stay ahead of the curve in educational practice, and the successful theological school in the 21st century cannot be an aloof, scholarly center to which students repair for a time before returning to the real world.

Conclusion

Of course, more could be said, but time will not allow it. Theological education in the 21st century must be responsive to the realities of the 21st century. Those laboring in theological education could do no better than to reflect in their own times, places, and styles concerning the innovative and forward-looking practices of Joseph and James Mathews in their lifetimes.

Postlude

In the year 2000, Jack Gilles and a large number of our colleagues responded to a long standing request from Lyn Mathews Edwards, by then deceased, to bring colleagues of EI/ICA together to look at what we were all doing and to review the challenges before us in the new millennium. From that event we all learned how busily engaged we were in a wide range of activities, meeting social needs and nurturing the human spirit. Since that time a series of events occurred, including several meetings in Denver, a meeting in 2007 at Abbey North in Canada, and 2008 at Lake Junaluska in North Carolina.

Out of this initial meeting, a series of regional meetings across the USA and others in Asia, resulted in establishing new collaborations, decisions to publish what we were doing and expanding the learning since Joseph Mathews died in 1977. Our intention is to extend our collaboration to look deeply at contemporary perspectives on the church and the demands of the social order.

As we pondered the future and our legacy, we coined the phrase "Springboard" for our network--a group that is not a monolithic organization or institution but more of a loosely-affiliated association. We intend to have periodic gatherings that would focus on how to capture what is most valuable from our heritage, what we are learning now and apply it to the demands upon us in this new century. Indeed our ranks have grown over the past 30 years to include many who know little of our legacy and origins.

Postlude

Prior to and flowing from these events have been numerous publications including those facilitated with Bishop James K. Mathews and the Mathews family: Bending History and Brother Joe. With the relocation of the Joe Mathews personal archives to Wesley Theological Seminary by the Mathews family, a whole new burst of energy and opportunity caused us to envision this Symposium as a way to both celebrate our heritage and to identify directions that we may share in common. This new impetus should guide us toward the future with thousands of colleagues around the world. Thus was born this Symposium, held in December, 2009.

We asked all those who registered for this Symposium to bring forth their best works in the forms of presentations and publishable papers and other media, and we recorded most of these sessions to glean their best wisdom regarding what continues to inspire and nurture us from our heritage. Following the Symposium, we have worked to produce these findings for publication, making them available to a wider audience.

The theme remains the same as that of the Symposium, "Transforming the Legacy: People of the Spirit in the 21st Century." This is *Volume I: The Legacy and the Challenges*; it serves as something of a "festschrift" as testimony to the work of the two Mathews brothers, but most of the papers here look forward to the challenges before us. Volume II will be entitled 'The Response and Emerging Directions' and include most of the remaining papers presented in the Symposium workshops, along with other papers on the workshop themes that people from the Springboard network are submitting.

Meanwhile, we also published a second edition of a booklet that Bishop Mathews had prepared in 1959 for the Woman's Division of Christian Service of the Board of Missions of the Methodist Church (now part of the General Board of Global Ministries of the United Methodist Church). That volume entitled *'Eternal Values in a World of Change'*, which includes at the end a sermon preached by Bishop Mathews as he accepted retirement from the active Episcopacy in 1980, had been long out of print, but it serves as a send-off for those of us who assume responsibility for doing church in the 21st century. It carries the same title as the original because it is immensely relevant today and is priced inexpensively so that it might gain wide usage among study groups who want to take seriously the continuing challenges lying before People of the Spirit.

ICAI with its many national affiliates and ICA at USA headquarters in Chicago carries on a flourishing program of consultations and social service initiatives. Most recently, in March 2010, approximately 40 colleagues, including guests from Canada, Botswana, Bangladesh, Nepal and the UK, attended a meeting that explored rekindling international program interest. The purpose of the gathering was to consider ideas about ways that ICA-USA might assist in connecting human and financial resources from the United States with national ICAs, and other projects, in developing nations.

The participants formulated a practical vision about ICA-USA's re-engagement in this area, reflected upon challenges, and worked through scenarios of possible action. Sue Laxdal, a ToP® colleague from Minnesota, facilitated the process. Roberston Work, recently retired from the United Nations Development Program (UNDP)--now teaching international development in New York and Malaysia--made a presentation about the current realities and urgency of global development. A video clip is available on the website: www.ica-usa.org, as is a summary of the proceedings of this March meeting. More information can be secured from the website, or by contacting Karen Sims at ksims@ica-usa.org.

In addition, one of our colleagues, John Cock, has put together a series of immersion events called The Profound Journey Dialog (PJD) that focuses on the deep journey of our lives. Utilizing universal, inclusive language and offering empowering images, the PJD offers tools for persons to care for themselves as they care for the world--from the local neighborhood to the entire Earth community.

The PJD is an interactive event, building on four master journey images. Consisting of brief presentations, large and small group dialog, meal conversations, time for personal reflection, short contextual readings, and secular-spiritual rituals, the four sessions can be exhilarating, intense, transforming and celebrative. The Profound Journey Dialog reiterates the underpinnings of the various methods of courses in the EI/ICA heritage, methods that continue to be used in groups all over the globe. The PJD events have motivated thousands to volunteer in efforts around the world, helping to transform lives and communities continuing for over 40 years.

Additionally, one of our Symposium Speakers, Mark Davies, Dean at the Petree College of Arts and Sciences, Oklahoma City University, and Co-Founder, Oikos, Inc. at OCU, a non-profit organization focuses on systemic solutions for global sustainability with special emphasis on the issues of peace and nonviolence, social justice and human need, and ecological sustainability. OKCU will be building an archive in conjunction with ICA-USA. Oikos already partners with the Division of Higher Education of the General Board of Higher Education and Ministry of the United Methodist Church to lead the Methodist Global Ethics Initiative--an effort to help United Methodist and other Methodist-related schools, colleges, and universities collaborate with one another to more effectively provide education for social and ecological responsibility. Mark will be holding another consultation in the near future that will move these projects along, and welcomes participation from anyone in our network. He can be reached at mdavies@okcu.edu; www.okcu.edu; www.oikosmovement.org

Those who read this account of the Symposium in 2009 may indeed experience that you are a part of the evolving global network of People of Spirit. We hope you will continue to participate and contribute. Please do that through any of the websites above or our website as noted below. On behalf of the Symposium Steering Committee--Dr. D. William Faupel, Dr. E. Maynard Moore, Jack Gilles, Susan Craver and I, we again wish to express our gratitude to Wesley Theological Seminary, the Mathews Family, and all the supporters and sponsors for making this 2009 event a reality. Most importantly we thank all those who attended the event to mark a significant moment in a long journey to serve a suffering world.

M. George Walters, Corporate Secretary
Resurgence Publishing Corporation
www.ResurgencePublishing.com

Volume II: The Response and Emerging Directions

The forthcoming companion to Volume I:

Volume II of *Transforming the Legacy: People of Spirit in the 21st Century* will be titled *'The Response and Emerging Directions'* and will present contributions from the workshop leaders and participants focused on the future. The workshop tracks look in depth at the legacy and the 21st century challenges set forth in Volume I and the response and future directions being charted now by People of Spirit.

In his keynote address William A. (Bill) Holmes said that the organizers of the event placed a heavy emphasis on the future directions that the People of Spirit in the 21st Century must identify and in which they must engage. The workshop Tracks served exactly this purpose with presentations, discussions and strategic thinking focused on six major challenge areas.

Track 1: Urban Mission
Track 2: Interfaith Engagement
Track 3: Educational Mandates
Track 4: Environmental Stewardship
Track 5: Global Health
Track 6: Corporate Ethics

Publication is scheduled for Quarter 4 2010

Resurgence Publishing Website (www.ResurgencePublishing.com) .

Host Sponsor: Wesley Theological Seminary

About Our Seminary

www.wesleyseminary.edu

Seated in the nation's capital, centered in Christian faith, Wesley Theological Seminary prepares over 1,000 students annually, representing more than 25 denominations, to become exemplary teachers, preachers, and leaders in the world today.

The mission of Wesley Theological Seminary is to equip Christians for leadership in the church and the world, to advance theological scholarship, and to model a prophetic voice in the public square. Wesley is a teaching seminary and a service-oriented community. Our graduates are in ministry in all 50 states and in 20 countries as leaders of churches and other service organizations.

Wesley has come to have a strong impact through its commitment to service and to congregational partnerships. As vectors of creative, collaborative and scholarly practice, the members of Wesley's 2009 graduating class alone will minister to more than half a million people in the course of their careers. I welcome you to join them.

The Rev. Dr. David McAllister-Wilson, President

J-Term
Master of Divinity
Master of Arts
Master of Theological Studies
Doctor of Ministry

Equipping Lay Ministry
National Capital Semester for Seminarians
Summer Term 2009
Center for Deacon Education
Course of Study

Host Sponsor: Wesley Theological Seminary

Urban Ministry:

Urban ministry at Wesley centers on contextual education. Based in downtown Washington, DC, and in partnership with two historic churches, Wesley's urban ministry students learn to engage the poor and the powerful, to meet the needs of diverse cultures, and to answer their call to dynamic, applied ministry in the complex social systems of the inner-city. Wesley's urban ministry program provides supervised study, specialized coursework, and an urban ministry placement. Coursework includes Introduction to Urban Ministry I & II, Sociology of Religion, Pastoral Care and Counseling in Context, and 9 elective credits from the urban ministry curriculum.

Urban Fellows Program:

Urban Fellows are outstanding Master of Divinity students who sense a calling to become leaders in urban ministry. They seek faithful solutions to the challenges of homelessness and gentrification, addiction, failed schools, inaccessible health care systems, unemployment, and illiteracy. And they enjoy exceptional opportunities to grow through internships with urban congregations, social service advocacy groups and not-for-profit organizations, as well as mentorships with experienced urban pastors and leaders. Urban Fellows receive scholarship funding and will have opportunities to: Urban Fellows will have opportunities to:

- Provide pastoral care and leadership in congregations and other settings
- Engage in community organizing & collaborative research projects
- Advocate and mobilize for justice issues
- Build connectivity amongst ecumenical and interfaith communities

How to Apply:

Interested students are encouraged to apply to the Urban Fellows program as part of their admissions process to Wesley. Urban Fellows are required to be full-time Master of Divinity students taking a minimum of 9 hours each semester. Applicants must submit an essay addressing the following questions:

- How have you experienced a call to Urban Ministry?
- What qualifications or experiences support your Urban Ministry calling?
- In what type of ministry setting do you see yourself serving in the future?

Essays of no more than 1500 words must be received no later than February 1. Essays may be submitted by email to admissions@wesleyseminary.edu, by fax to attn: Admissions at (202) 885-8585 or by mail to Admissions Office, Wesley Theological Seminary, 4500 Massachusetts Ave NW, Washington, DC, 20016. Finalists for the Urban Fellows program will be invited to interview with members of the Urban Ministry Faculty Committee.

Intentional Living Community:

18 Wesley students live in intentional community in the heart of Washington, DC. The community intends that members grow spiritually while fostering relationships with one another and within the broader community through relevant engagement and faithful service. Select mentors will provide ongoing guidance in the process and experience. The intentional community is located at 900 Massachusetts Ave, NW. This area is characterized by tourism, power, and poverty: expensive condominiums; low-income residential neighborhoods; the convention center; homeless shelters; and law firms. Capitol Hill, the White House, Smithsonian museums, and the vibrant Chinatown business district all lie in the surrounding blocks. All Wesley students who feel called to intentional community may apply, regardless of degree program. To be eligible, students must be enrolled as full-time students at Wesley while living in the community. All students selected to live at Mt. Vernon Place will receive support to cover a portion of actual housing expenses.

Author Profiles

Rev. Bruce C. Birch, Ph.D.

Emeritus Dean and Woodrow W. and Mildred B. Miller Emeritus Professor of Biblical Theology at Wesley Theological Seminary, Washington, D.C. A native of Kansas, Bruce received his B.A. from Southwestern College, his B.D. from Perkins School of Theology at Southern Methodist University and his Ph.D. from Yale University. He did post-doctoral study at Tübingen University in West Germany. He taught at Yale, Iowa Wesleyan College and Erskine College (South Carolina) before coming to Wesley in 1971. Bruce is an ordained United Methodist minister in the Baltimore-Washington Annual Conference. He has been a delegate to General and Jurisdictional Conferences of the United Methodist Church and served on its General Board of Church and Society. He has lectured and consulted in a wide range of academic and church settings and for numerous ecumenical events. He serves on the Council of the Society of Biblical Literature, currently serving as its chairperson. A frequent contributor to journals and periodicals, he has authored numerous books. He was originating editor and a contributor to The Discipleship Study Bible and is currently translating 1 and 2 Samuel for the Common English Bible, a new translation under preparation by Abingdon Press. Contact information: bbirch@wesleyseminary.edu

Rabbi Fred Scherlinder Dobb

Rabbi, Adat Shalom Reconstructionist Congregation in Bethesda, Md. Chair of the Greater Washington Interfaith Power and Light steering committee, and a long-time lay-leader in the Coalition on the Environment and Jewish Life (and in 2003-04 the first rabbi on COEJL staff), Fred is also active with the Shalom Center (Philadelphia), Religious Witness for the Earth, and other Jewish and interfaith efforts. Fred just received his Doctor of Ministry from Wesley Theological Seminary, having written on "Sustained Sustainability: Eco-Judaism from the Pulpit, Enriched with Interfaith Intersections"; he lives in Washington D.C. with his wife Minna, pre-K daughter Sara, and baby son Gilad. Dobb is the first full-time Rabbi of Adat Shalom Reconstructionist Congregation, a dynamic 490-household synagogue in the Washington D.C. area (www.adatshalom.net). The congregation built its own EPA-Energy-Star-Award-winning building; and gained visibility and respect nationally and in the greater Washington community. Dobb was ordained in 1997 from Philadelphia's Reconstructionist Rabbinical College. A Wexner Graduate Fellow, Fred graduated in 1992 from Brandeis University (summa cum laude) and in 1992-93 he studied at the Pardes

Institute for Jewish Studies in Jerusalem. Dobb is a Past President of the Washington Board of Rabbis, and has served on the Boards of the InterFaith Conference of Metropolitan Washington, the Jewish Community Council of Greater Washington, and the Reconstructionist Rabbinical Association. Long interested in Judaism and social justice, Fred is involved with DC's *Shomrei Adamah*, Jews United for Justice, and other local groups. Contact information: rabbifred@adatshalom.net

Rev. Dr. William A. Holmes

United Methodist Baltimore-Washington Conference (retired), Silver Spring, Md. Bill Holmes began his career in 1955 as associate minister at Highland Park United Methodist Church, and went on to serve as minister of Northaven UMC in Dallas, as senior minister at the University UMC in Austin, Texas, and as minister of preaching and administration at the national United Methodist Church, Metropolitan Memorial, in Washington D.C. He retired in 1998. Holmes graduated from Hendrix College in Conway, Ark., earned a Master of Divinity from Perkins School of Theology at SMU, and continued postgraduate studies at Union Theological Seminary in New York City. In addition, he was awarded a Doctor of Divinity Degree in 1970 by Southwestern University in Georgetown, Tx., and a Doctor of Humane Letters in 1978 from Western Maryland College in Westminster, Md. He is married to Nancy Murray, and they have two grown children, Will and Chris, and six grandchildren. Holmes first came to national prominence following a sermon preached at Northaven Church two days after the assassination of President John F. Kennedy. Excerpts from this sermon were carried on the "CBS Walter Cronkite Evening News," and served as the framework for a Chapter in A Man Named John F. Kennedy (Paulist Press). Holmes has been featured as preacher on The Protestant Hour, and has delivered keynote speeches at Perkins School of Theology, Duke Divinity School, Boston University School of Theology, Wesley Theological Seminary, and Candler School of Theology at Emory University. Holmes has served as a member of the Governing Board of the National Council of Churches, U.S.A., and as a trustee at The American University, Western Maryland College, and Sibley Memorial Hospital. He was a student of Joseph Wesley Mathews at Perkins, and served for some years as a trainer and speaker through the Christian Faith and Life Community in Austin. Contact information: bilnanh@msn.com

Rev. Clark Lobenstine

Executive Director of the InterFaith Conference (IFC) of Metropolitan Washington D.C. Clark began his role with the IFC in April, 1979 and recently celebrated his 30th anniversary as Executive Director. The InterFaith Conference was the first staffed organization in the world which brought together the Islamic, Jewish, Protestant and Roman Catholic faith communities both to deepen understanding and to build a just community in a metropolitan area. The vision of its three founders, including Bishop James K. Mathews, continues to guide this inter-religious organization today, even as its membership has grown to include 11 world religions – Baha'i, Buddhist, Hindu, Islamic, Jain, Jewish, Latter-day Saints, Protestant, Roman Catholic, Sikh and Zoroastrian faith communities in this region. Rev. Dr. Lobenstine's thesis-article for his Doctor of Ministry degree from McCormick Seminary was on Christian-Muslim relations. He was a participant in the first international interfaith dialogue hosted by the Custodian of the Two Holy Mosques last summer in Madrid and participated with his wife in the follow-up dialogue in Geneva this fall. Clark is also Parish Associate (volunteer assistant minister) at the Silver Spring Presbyterian Church in Maryland. He is a founding member of the Washington Metropolitan Dialogue and the Secretary of D.C. Mayor Adrian Fenty's Interfaith Council. He is married to The Rev. Carole A. Crumley and they have three grandchildren. Clark is a twin, has twin sons and twin nieces. clarkifc@ifcmw.org

Bishop Felton Edwin May

Bishop (retired), the United Methodist Church; Riverdale, N.Y. Felton Edwin May grew up in Chicago. After receiving a B.A. from Judson College he was ordained a deacon in the Northern Illinois Conference and served two appointments in Chicago: St. James Church and Maple Park Church, a new church start. Throughout the 'sixties, he was active in the movement for housing opportunity, educational equality, and the campaign for jobs and justice led by Dr. Martin L. King, Jr., Rev. Jesse Jackson, and local leaders on Chicago's Southwest side. In 1968, he transferred to the Peninsula Annual Conference where he served as associate executive director of the Methodist Action Program in Wilmington, Del., from 1968-1970. In 1970, he was ordained elder by Bishop John Wesley Lord after receiving an M.Div. Degree from Crozer Theological Seminary. In the Peninsula Conference, he also served as pastor, as superintendent of the Easton District under Bishop James K. Mathews (1975-1981), and as director of the Conference Council on Ministries (1981-1984). He was a delegate to the Northeastern Jurisdictional Conference on four occasions, and a delegate to General Conference three times. Elected to the Episcopacy in 1984, he served the Harrisburg Episcopal Area in Pennsylvania from 1984 to 1996. In 1996, he was assigned to the National Capital Episcopal Area. After retirement in September 2004, he accepted the position as Dean of the Harry R.

Kendall Science and Health Mission Center at Philander Smith College, Little Rock, Ark. In 1990, May served as Bishop-on-Special Assignment to organize and coordinate the United Methodist Bishops' Initiative on Drug and Alcohol Abuse and Violence in Washington, D.C. He is the only United Methodist bishop asked by the Council of Bishops to leave an Episcopal Area to serve a special assignment on its behalf, and then return to active service. Bishop May has served as a member of the General Council on Ministries (1984-1992), the General Board of Global Ministries (1992-2000), and the General Board of Higher Education and Ministry (2000 to present). He was president of the General Council on Ministries from 1988 to 1992, and Vice President of the General Board of Global Ministries 1996 – 2000. He has also served as chair of the National Shalom Zone Committee, the Special Program on Substance Abuse and Related Violence, the Commission on Pan-Methodist Cooperation, the General Board of Global Ministries' Finance Committee, the Northeastern Jurisdiction Board of the Multi-Ethnic Center, the Advance for Christ and His Church Committee, and the Council of Bishops' Emerging Issues Committee. In 1999, Bishop May served as a member of the White House Presidential Mission on Children Orphaned by AIDS, traveling with that group to Africa. He was also a participant in the White House's Faith Leaders for "One America Initiative," the UN Millennium World Peace Summit of Religious and Spiritual Leaders, and the Camp David Presidential Retreat Interfaith Chapel Committee. Bishop May now serves as Vice President of the Board of Directors of Africa University, teaches and preaches frequently in Africa. He has received honorary degrees from Lebanon Valley College, Lycoming College, Wesley College and Rusk College. He lives now with wife Phyllis in Riverdale, N.Y. Contact information: fepe2328@comcast.net

Rev. David McAllister-Wilson

President, Wesley Theological Seminary, Washington, D.C. McAllister-Wilson assumed the office of President at Wesley Theological Seminary on July 1, 2002. He has served the institution for over 25 years, beginning in Wesley's Development Office as a fundraiser, and later as Executive Vice President. During that period, he was part of a team that made Wesley one of the nation's largest and leading theological schools, preparing approximately 1,300 men and women for ministry each year. McAllister-Wilson has focused his preaching and speaking in an effort to help revitalize the Mainline Protestant Church, helping to encourage men and women to consider God's call to ministry and preparing them for leadership. With a strong interest and focus on leadership development, particularly in local congregations, he helped to establish the G.

Douglass Lewis Center for Church Leadership at Wesley. An active, lifelong United Methodist, he is originally from Thousand Oaks, Cal. With a strong leadership focus on community ministry work, he established the Community Conscience Foundation, a foundation that supported local human services agencies. He has remained actively involved as a consultant and board member with community-based human service agencies. Now a member of the Virginia Annual Conference, McAllister-Wilson was ordained Deacon in 1988 and Elder in 1993. David has always had a passion for the training and development of effective leadership and has coauthored the book, Christian Reflections on the Leadership Challenge. McAllister-Wilson received a Bachelor of Arts in History from California State University, Northridge, in 1983. He earned his Master of Divinity (1988) and Doctor of Ministry (2001) degrees from Wesley Theological Seminary. He is married to The Reverend Drema McAllister-Wilson who formerly served as Pastor of Fairlington United Methodist Church in Alexandria, Virginia, and now serves as Chaplain at the Washington Community Hospices in Washington, DC. Contact information: mbates@wesleyseminary.edu: www.wesleyseminary.edu

Rev. E. Maynard Moore, Ph.D.

Principal/Partner of Community Nexus Consulting, LLC, Bethesda, Maryland. Maynard is a member of the Baltimore-Washington Conference (retired) and actively teaches various classes in Science & Religion at Metropolitan Memorial United Methodist Church in Washington D.C. He served from 2003-2005 as Executive Co-Director for the Stewardship Center and Foundation of the Baltimore-Washington Conference of the United Methodist Church. He has participated in various conferences in Science and Religion, including the 2002 Symposium with the Dalai Lama at M.I.T., the Science and Human Quest Conference at Harvard University, and others organized under the auspices of the Center for Theology and the Natural Sciences in Berkeley, Cal. He has consulted with a wide variety of nonprofit organizations, including Habitat for Humanity International, the Minority Health Professions Foundation, the World Mental Health Association, and more than two dozen colleges and universities. He holds degrees from Randolph-Macon College, Perkins School of Theology, Southern Methodist University, the University of Chicago Divinity School, and the Union Institute & University in Cincinnati, Ohio. He first took courses at the Christian Faith & Life Community in Austin while in seminary, and it was while serving as Dean at the Central YMCA Community College in Chicago in the 1970s that he first got involved with the Ecumenical Institute. He now lives in Bethesda with his wife, Paula, who conducts an orchestra for people with mental &

physical disabilities. Contact information: emaynard8@yahoo.com; www.comm-nex.com

Bishop Susan M. Morrison

Bishop (retired), The United Methodist Church; Rehoboth Beach, Del. Susan Morrison was born in Dunkirk, N.Y. After graduation from Drew University, she spent three and a half years as a short-term missionary in Brazil. Returning to the States, she studied for a M.Div. degree at Boston University School of Theology, graduating magna cum laude. Her Doctor of Ministry degree was earned at Wesley Theological Seminary. She has also studied in London, Rome, Buenos Aires and Cuernavaca, Mexico. Susan was ordained a deacon by Bishop John Wesley Lord in the Peninsula Conference, December 6, 1970 and an elder in the Baltimore-Washington Conference by Bishop James K. Mathews on May 30, 1974. She served pastorates at Marvin Memorial United Methodist Church in Silver Spring, Md., and Emmanuel United Methodist Church in Beltsville, Md. In 1980 she was appointed by Bishop Mathews as Superintendent of the Baltimore Northwest District, during which time she served for one year as Dean of the Cabinet. In 1986, she was appointed Council Director of the Baltimore Washington Annual Conference. She served as chair of the committee that developed the current Book of Worship of the United Methodist Church. At the 1988 General Conference Susan was elected to the Judicial Council. The Northeastern Jurisdictional Conference of 1988 then elected her to the episcopacy and she was assigned to the Philadelphia Area, where she served for eight years. In 1996, she was assigned to the Albany Area, serving there until her retirement in 2006. Susan now lives in Rehoboth Beach, Del. Contact information: ogn509@aol.com

Bishop John R. Schol

Presiding Bishop, the National Capital Area, The United Methodist Church. The Washington Episcopal Area, includes over 690 United Methodist congregations with more than 200,000 members in Maryland, Washington, D.C., and the eastern panhandle of West Virginia. He took office Sept. 1, 2004, after being elected a bishop of The United Methodist Church in Syracuse, N.Y., July 16, 2004. At the time, he was serving as pastor of the West Chester United Methodist Church in Pennsylvania. Prior to that he served as Urban Ministry Executive Secretary and Communities of Shalom Director for the General Board of Global Ministries in New York. There, he helped start and direct the Communities of Shalom ministry and the Holy Boldness initiative that became a national training academy in urban ministry. He began in Los Angeles, addressing the issues and needs of a community recovering from riots following racial unrest. Today the Shalom movement encompasses 530 sites in 42 annual conferences in the United States, Zimbabwe and Ghana, with more than 6,000 people trained. Beginning in 1981 and for the next twelve years Schol served as Executive Director and Pastor of the Frankford Group Ministry in Philadelphia. Schol is a graduate of Moravian College in Bethlehem, Penna., and holds his M.Div and D. Min. degrees from Boston University, where he graduated *magna cum laude* in 1995. Schol has been honored on several occasions with Human Relations awards and was recognized by the Mayor of Philadelphia with the Liberty Bell Award. He has served as program chair of the Northeastern Jurisdiction Multi-Ethnic Center and also for the United Methodist Metro Ministries team. As a delegate from the Eastern Pennsylvania Conference to the 2004 General Conference of the United Methodist Church, Schol was instrumental in developing a resolution that avoided a possible division of the church. John also has served as a delegate to the World Methodist Council, and served as Co-Chair of Hope for the Children of Africa. He spearheads the current United Methodist-sponsored "Nothing but Nets" program that has made significant strides in abating the spread of malaria in East Africa. He has provided leadership and lay training in over 150 urban and rural communities in the United States, Mexico, Kenya and Zimbabwe. John is married to Beverly Anne; they have three children. Contact: bishopsoffice@BWCUMC.org

John Silber, Ph.D.

President Emeritus of Boston University and Professor of International Relations, Law, and Philosophy. (B.A. Trinity University; M.A., Ph.D., Yale University). Dr. Silber is an internationally recognized authority on ethics, on the philosophy of law, and on the philosophy of Immanuel Kant. His works include: The Ethical Significance of Kant's Religion; Being and Doing: A Study of Status Responsibility and Voluntary Responsibility; Human Action and the Language of Volition; Procedural Formalism in Kant's Ethics; The Natural Good and the Moral Good in Kant's Ethics; Obedience to the Unenforceable. His book Straight Shooting: What's Wrong with America and How to Fix It, was published in 1989. A German edition, *Ist Amerika zu retten?*, was published in 1992 and a Japanese edition was published in 1993. In 2007 his book Architecture of the Absurd: How Genius Disfigured a Practical Art was published. Silber is a leading spokesman for the maintenance of high academic standards and has gained national attention for his advocacy of a rational, comprehensive system for financing higher education. In January 1996, Governor William Weld chose Professor Silber to head the Massachusetts Board of Education, the state's policy-making board for public education at the elementary, middle and high school levels. He continues his writing and correspondence from his home in Boston.

Joseph A. Slicker

Member of Order/Ecumenical, now living in Dallas, Texas. Joe was born on December 1, 1920 in West Central Texas and reared in Cisco, 10 miles to the west. He obtained Bachelor of Science degrees in Petroleum and Mechanical engineering from Texas A. & M. He was an army officer in Antiaircraft serving in the Pacific Theater during WWII. He served on several islands ending with the Iwo Jima invasion, an experience that "jerked the world out from under me." After the war ended he began work as a Petroleum Engineer for eight years during which time he married Anne Cook of Texarkana resulting later in three children. He made the decision to enter the Presbyterian ministry, and both he and Anne attended seminary, taking later a parish assignment in an expanding suburb. Within a year, Joe and Anne relocated to Austin to work with college students at the Christian Faith & Life Community, and then were part of the team transferring to Chicago to the Ecumenical Institute, whose work later expanded to non-religious groups as The Institute of Cultural Affairs. As the work developed world-wide, Joe and Anne lived in India for three years and Kenya for five. During the 80s, Joe and Anne moved back to Chicago where they worked primarily in expanding the ICA basic curriculum. Joe continued the practice of meditation and during this time he expanded it with work in the Kabalah. Anne began using Silva Mind Control Meditation. They retired in 1989 and moved to Dallas, Texas, where they now live in a retirement home called Edgemere with a life affirming staff of caregivers, a place, in Joe's words, *"where one can wake up, become aware that life itself is good in its wholeness, and see the triumphant aspect of living and dying."*

Rev. Fred Smith, Ph.D.

Associate Professor of Urban Ministry and Associate Director of the Practice of Ministry and Mission, Wesley Theological Seminary, Washington, D.C. Fred formerly served as pastor of Fellowship United Methodist Church in Ambridge, Penna., and served as Associate Professor of Christian Education and Youth Ministry, & Director of the Lilly Endowment-funded Summer Youth Institute at Pittsburgh Theological Seminary. Previously he was, for seven years, Associate Director of the Interfaith Health Program at the Carter Presidential Center in Atlanta, Ga. Educated at Harvard College (B.A. '73), Perkins School of Theology of Southern Methodist University (M.Div. cum laude '84) and Emory University

(Ph.D. '97), he has directed a number national initiatives including: Consultant to the United Methodist Council of Bishop's Initiative on Children and Poverty, Pan-Methodist Coalition on Alcohol and Drug Abuse; The Carnegie Foundation's Kids and Guns Initiative; National Volunteer Training Centers' National Interfaith Alliance Against Substance Abuse; The Southern Christian Leadership Conference's Stop the Killing Campaign, and The Carter Center's Whole Communities Collaborative. He has authored or coauthored many books, articles, and reports such as: Black Religious Experience: Conversation or Double Consciousness, "A Prophetic Religious Education for Y2K and Beyond: And Black Boys Shall See Visions," in Theological Literacy for the Twenty-First Century, Ed. Rodney Petersen and Nancy M. Rourke; "Black-on-Black Violence: The Intramediation of Desire and the Search for a Scapegoat," in Contagion: Journal of Violence, Mimesis and Culture; The Revival of Hope: Faith-based Substance Abuse Curriculum (Cokesbury); Not Even One: A Report on the Crisis of Children and Firearms (The Carter Center); "Violence as Public Health Issue for African American Youth" in The Caregiver Journal; "The Role of the Faith Community," in Community Links. Contact information: fsmith@wesleyseminary.edu

Rev. Dr. Dean Snyder

Senior Pastor of Foundry United Methodist Church, Washington, D.C. Under Dean's leadership, since 2002, Foundry Church, a vital and diverse downtown congregation, has continued and expanded a tradition of engagement in community ministries, including outreach to homeless persons, day laborers, and people living with HIV/AIDS. The church has set as one of its goals to lead a movement to end chronic homelessness in Washington, D.C., and by 2004. Foundry was also instrumental in the founding of the Union de Trabalhos of Washington D.C. and the Baltimore-Washington Area Reconciling Ministries (B-WARM). Snyder has ridden in several HIV-AIDS benefit rides. A popular preacher and public speaker, Snyder has preached at St. Paul's Cathedral and Wesley Chapel in London, and has served as conference preacher for United Methodist Annual Conferences in New Jersey and Liberia. Snyder serves on the Board of Ordained Ministry of the Baltimore-Washington Conference of the United Methodist Church and was the first editor of the conference's Adventure Guide. He has chaired the United Methodist Campus Ministry Board at American University. Prior to becoming senior pastor of Foundry Church, Snyder served as Director of Communications and Associate Council Director for Congregational Development for the Baltimore-Washington Conference. He is widely traveled in Africa and Central America, training new leaders in organizational development and community organizing theory and methodologies. Before joining the Baltimore-Washington Conference, Snyder served as campus minister to and taught at Drexel University, and pastored three urban congregations in Philadelphia, including a primarily African-American congregation and a downtown congregation whose members spanned more than twenty different ethnic groups. Dean studied at Albright College and Boston University School of Theology, and has done doctoral-level coursework with a focus on multiculturalism at the Howard University Divinity School. He was awarded an honorary Doctor of Divinity degree by Albright College in 2005. He is married to Jane Malone, a housing advocate, and has three children: David, a software developer and writer, Nancy, an early childhood educator in Guatemala, and Naomi, a marketing specialist. Contact information: dsnyder@foundryumc.org

Rev. M. George Walters, Resurgence Publishing Corporation

Corporate Secretary, Resurgence Publishing Corporation, Lutz, Florida. George Walters joined the Staff of the Ecumenical Institute with his wife, Carol, in 1967 as interns, and became a member of the National Teaching Faculty. Prior to that he worked for the National Council of Churches, Division of Christian Life and Mission, Commission on Religion and Race, as director of the Student Interracial Ministry while completing his M Div degree and graduating *magna cum laude* from Union Theological Seminary, NYC. After 24 years with the EI/ICA principally focused on international program research, he entered the private sector as an IT professional in 1991 and in 2004 formed Resurgence Publishing Corporation with 5 other colleagues to work with members of the Mathews family to publish works from the Archives of Joseph Wesley Mathews and to find a home for Joe's Archives which have now been gifted to Wesley Theological Seminary, Washington DC. www.ResurgencePublishing.com

Timothy Leonard Watson, NCARB

Principal, TLW Architect, Hillsborough, N.C. Tim principally serves as an "EcoRestorative Design" architect specializing in teaching and designing "Living Systems" whereby humans and nonhumans coexist symbiotically. He is committed to a new form of architecture that produces ecological rejuvenation of soil, rainwater flows, and people. He sees buildings as serving as humane, ecorestorative contributors to the natural world. His inspiration springs from indigenous people's belief in the sanctity of the Earth. Contact: www.tlwarchitect.com twblackeagle@earthlink.net

Breinigsville, PA USA
12 September 2010

245198BV00001B/3/P

9 780976 389248